Practical Synthetic Data Generation
Balancing Privacy and the
Broad Availability of Data

Khaled El Emam, Lucy Mosquera,
and Richard Hoptroff

Beijing · Boston · Farnham · Sebastopol · Tokyo

Practical Synthetic Data Generation

by Khaled El Emam, Lucy Mosquera, and Richard Hoptroff

Copyright © 2020 K Sharp Technology Inc., Lucy Mosquera, and Richard Hoptroff. All rights reserved.

Published by O'Reilly Media, Inc., 1005 Gravenstein Highway North, Sebastopol, CA 95472.

O'Reilly books may be purchased for educational, business, or sales promotional use. Online editions are also available for most titles (*http://oreilly.com*). For more information, contact our corporate/institutional sales department: 800-998-9938 or *corporate@oreilly.com*.

Acquisitions Editor: Jonathan Hassell	**Indexer:** Potomac Indexing, LLC
Development Editor: Corbin Collins	**Interior Designer:** David Futato
Production Editor: Christopher Faucher	**Cover Designer:** Karen Montgomery
Copyeditor: Piper Editorial	**Illustrator:** Jenny Bergman
Proofreader: JM Olejarz	

May 2020:   First Edition

Revision History for the First Edition

2020-05-19:   First Release

See *http://oreilly.com/catalog/errata.csp?isbn=9781492072744* for release details.

978-1-492-07274-4

[LSI]

Table of Contents

Preface

Interest in synthetic data has been growing rapidly over the last few years. This interest has been driven by two simultaneous trends. The first is the demand for large amounts of data to train and build artificial intelligence and machine learning (AIML) models. The second is recent work that has demonstrated effective methods for generating high-quality synthetic data. Both have resulted in the recognition that synthetic data can solve some difficult problems quite effectively, especially within the AIML community. Companies like NVIDIA, IBM, and Alphabet, as well as agencies such as the US Census Bureau, have adopted different types of data synthesis methodologies to support model building, application development, and data dissemination.

This book provides you with a gentle introduction to methods for the following: generating synthetic data, evaluating the data that has been synthesized, understanding the privacy implications of synthetic data, and implementing synthetic data within your organization. We show how synthetic data can accelerate AIML projects. Some of the problems that can be tackled by having synthetic data would be too costly or dangerous to solve using more traditional methods (e.g., training models controlling autonomous vehicles), or simply cannot be done otherwise. We also explain how to assess the privacy risks from synthetic data, even though they tend to be minimal if synthesis is done properly.

While we want this book to be an introduction, we also want it to be applied. Therefore, we will discuss some of the issues that will be encountered with real data, not curated or cleaned data. Real data is complex and messy, and data synthesis needs to be able to work within that context.

Our intended audience is analytics leaders who are responsible for enabling AIML model development and application within their organizations, as well as data scientists who want to learn how data synthesis can be a useful tool for their work. We will use examples of different types of data synthesis to illustrate the broad applicability of this approach. Our main focus here is on the synthesis of structured data.

Conventions Used in This Book

The following typographical conventions are used in this book:

Italic

Indicates new terms, URLs, email addresses, filenames, and file extensions.

O'Reilly Online Learning

 For more than 40 years, *O'Reilly Media* has provided technology and business training, knowledge, and insight to help companies succeed.

Our unique network of experts and innovators share their knowledge and expertise through books, articles, and our online learning platform. O'Reilly's online learning platform gives you on-demand access to live training courses, in-depth learning paths, interactive coding environments, and a vast collection of text and video from O'Reilly and 200+ other publishers. For more information, visit *http://oreilly.com*.

How to Contact Us

Please address comments and questions concerning this book to the publisher:

O'Reilly Media, Inc.
1005 Gravenstein Highway North
Sebastopol, CA 95472
800-998-9938 (in the United States or Canada)
707-829-0515 (international or local)
707-829-0104 (fax)

We have a web page for this book, where we list errata, examples, and any additional information. You can access this page at *https://oreil.ly/practical-synthetic-data-generation*.

Email *bookquestions@oreilly.com* to comment or ask technical questions about this book.

For news and information about our books and courses, visit *http://oreilly.com*.

Find us on Facebook: *http://facebook.com/oreilly*

Follow us on Twitter: *http://twitter.com/oreillymedia*

Watch us on YouTube: *http://youtube.com/oreillymedia*

Acknowledgments

The preparation of this book benefited from a series of interviews with subject matter experts. I would like to thank the following individuals for making themselves available to discuss their experiences and thoughts on the synthetic data market and technology: Fernanda Foertter, Jim Karkanias, Alexei Pozdnoukhov, Rev Lebaradian, John Ashley, Rob Csonger, and Simson Garfinkel.

Rob Csonger and his team provided the content for the section on autonomous vehicles.

Mike Hintze from Hintze Law LLC prepared the legal analysis in the identity disclosure chapter.

We wish to thank Janice Branson for reviewing earlier versions of the manuscript.

Our clients and collaborators, who often give us challenging problems, have been key to driving our innovations in the methods of data synthesis and the implementation of the technology in practice.

CHAPTER 1

Introducing Synthetic Data Generation

We start this chapter by explaining what synthetic data is and its benefits. Artificial intelligence and machine learning (AIML) projects run in various industries, and the use cases that we include in this chapter are intended to give a flavor of the broad applications of data synthesis. We define an AIML project quite broadly as well, to include, for example, the development of software applications that have AIML components.

Defining Synthetic Data

At a conceptual level, synthetic data is not real data, but data that has been generated from real data and that has the same statistical properties as the real data. This means that if an analyst works with a synthetic dataset, they should get analysis results similar to what they would get with real data. The degree to which a synthetic dataset is an accurate proxy for real data is a measure of *utility*. We refer to the process of generating synthetic data as *synthesis*.

Data in this context can mean different things. For example, data can be *structured* data, as one would see in a relational database. Data can also be *unstructured* text, such as doctors' notes, transcripts of conversations or online interactions by email or chat. Furthermore, images, videos, audio, and virtual environments are types of data that can be synthesized. Using machine learning, it is possible to create realistic pictures of people who do not exist in the real world (*https://oreil.ly/clu_p*).

There are three types of synthetic data. The first type is generated from actual/real datasets, the second type does not use real data, and the third type is a hybrid of these two. Let's examine them here.

Synthesis from Real Data

The first type of synthetic data is synthesized from real datasets. This means that the analyst has some real datasets and then builds a model to capture the distributions and structure of that real data. Here *structure* means the multivariate relationships and interactions in the data. Once the model is built, the synthetic data is sampled or generated from that model. If the model is a good representation of the real data, then the synthetic data will have statistical properties similar to those of the real data.

This is illustrated in Figure 1-1. Here we fit the data to a generative model first. This captures the relationships in the data. We then use that model to generate synthetic data. So the synthetic data is produced from the fitted model.

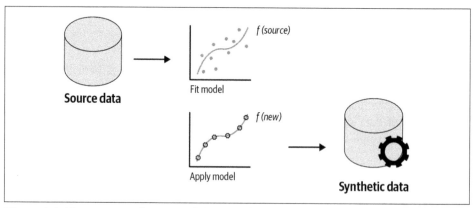

Figure 1-1. The conceptual process of data synthesis

For example, a data science group specializing in understanding customer behaviors would need large amounts of data to build its models. But because of privacy or other concerns, the process for accessing that customer data is slow and does not provide good enough data on account of extensive masking and redaction of information. Instead, a synthetic version of the production datasets can be provided to the analysts to build their models with. The synthesized data will have fewer constraints on its use and will allow them to progress more rapidly.

Synthesis Without Real Data

The second type of synthetic data is not generated from real data. It is created by using existing models or the analyst's background knowledge.

These existing models can be statistical models of a process (developed through surveys or other data collection mechanisms) or they can be simulations. Simulations can be, for instance, gaming engines that create simulated (and synthetic) images of scenes or objects, or they can be simulation engines that generate shopper data with particular characteristics (say, age and gender) for people who walk past a store at different times of the day.

Background knowledge can be, for example, knowledge of how a financial market behaves that comes from textbook descriptions or the movements of stock prices under various historical conditions. It can also be knowledge of the statistical distribution of human traffic in a store based on years of experience. In such a case, it is relatively straightforward to create a model and sample from background knowledge to generate synthetic data. If the analyst's knowledge of the process is accurate, then the synthetic data will behave in a manner that is consistent with real-world data. Of course, the use of background knowledge works only when the analyst truly understands the phenomenon of interest.

As a final example, when a process is new or not well understood by the analyst, and there is no real historical data to use, then an analyst can make some simple assumptions about the distributions and correlations among the variables involved in the process. For example, the analyst can make a simplifying assumption that the variables have normal distributions and "medium" correlations among them, and create data that way. This type of data will likely not have the same properties as real data but can still be useful for some purposes, such as debugging an R data analysis program, or some types of performance testing of software applications.

Synthesis and Utility

For some use cases, having high utility will matter quite a bit. In other cases, medium or even low utility may be acceptable. For example, if the objective is to build AIML models to predict customer behavior and make marketing decisions based on that, then high utility will be important. On the other hand, if the objective is to see if your software can handle a large volume of transactions, then the data utility expectations will be considerably lower. Therefore, understanding what data, models, simulators, and knowledge exist, as well as the requirements for data utility, will drive the specific approach for generating the synthetic data.

A summary of the synthetic data types is given in Table 1-1.

Table 1-1. Different types of data synthesis with their utility implications

Type of synthetic data	Utility
Generated from real nonpublic datasets	Can be quite high
Generated from real public data	Can be high, although there are limitations because public data tends to be de-identified or aggregated
Generated from an existing model of a process, which can also be represented in a simulation engine	Will depend on the fidelity of the existing generating model
Based on analyst knowledge	Will depend on how well the analyst knows the domain and the complexity of the phenomenon

Type of synthetic data	Utility
Generated from generic assumptions not specific to the phenomenon	Will likely be low

Now that you have seen the different types of synthetic data, let's look at the benefits of data synthesis overall and of some of these data types specifically.

The Benefits of Synthetic Data

We will highlight two important benefits of data synthesis: providing more efficient access to data and enabling better analytics. Let's examine each of these in turn.

Efficient Access to Data

Data access is critical to AIML projects. The data is needed to train and validate models. More broadly, data is also needed for evaluating AIML technologies that have been developed by others, as well as for testing AIML software applications or applications that incorporate AIML models.

Typically, data is collected for a particular purpose with the consent of the individual —for example, for participating in a webinar or a clinical research study. If you want to use that same data for a different purpose, such as to build a model to predict what kind of person is likely to sign up for a webinar or to participate in a clinical study, then that is considered a secondary purpose.

Access to data for secondary purposes, such as analysis, is becoming problematic. The Government Accountability Office[1] and the McKinsey Global Institute[2] both note that accessing data for building and testing AIML models is a challenge for their adoption more broadly. A Deloitte analysis concluded that data-access issues are ranked in the top three challenges faced by companies when implementing AI.[3] At the same time, the public is getting uneasy about how its data is used and shared, and privacy laws are becoming stricter. A recent survey by O'Reilly highlighted the privacy concerns of companies adopting machine learning models, with more than half of companies experienced with AIML checking for privacy issues.[4]

Contemporary privacy regulations, such as the US Health Insurance Portability and Accountability Act (HIPAA) and the General Data Protection Regulation (GDPR) in

---

1 US Government Accountability Office, "Artificial Intelligence: Emerging Opportunities, Challenges, and Implications for Policy and Research" (March 2018) *https://www.gao.gov/products/GAO-18-644T*.

2 McKinsey Global Institute, "Artificial intelligence: The next digital frontier?", June 2017. *https://oreil.ly/pFMkl*.

3 Deloitte Insights, "State of AI in the Enterprise, 2nd Edition" 2018. *https://oreil.ly/EiD6T*.

4 Ben Lorica and Paco Nathan, *The State of Machine Learning Adoption in the Enterprise* (Sebastopol: O'Reilly, 2018).

Europe, require a legal basis to use personal data for a secondary purpose. An example of that legal basis would be additional consent or authorization from individuals before their data can be used. In many cases this is not practical and can introduce bias into the data because consenters and nonconsenters differ on important characteristics.[5]

Given the difficulty of accessing data, sometimes analysts try to just use open source or public datasets. These can be a good starting point, but they lack diversity and are often not well matched to the problems that the models are intended to solve. Furthermore, open data may lack sufficient heterogeneity for robust training of models. For example, open data may not capture rare cases well enough.

Data synthesis can give the analyst, rather efficiently and at scale, realistic data to work with. Synthetic data would not be considered identifiable personal data. Therefore, privacy regulations would not apply and additional consent to use the data for secondary purposes would not be necessary.[6]

Enabling Better Analytics

A use case where synthesis can be applied is when real data does not exist—for example, if the analyst is trying to model something completely new, and the creation or collection of a real dataset from scratch would be cost-prohibitive or impractical. Synthesized data can also cover edge or rare cases that are difficult, impractical, or unethical to collect in the real world.

Sometimes real data exists but is not labeled. Labeling a large amount of examples for supervised learning tasks can be time-consuming, and manual labeling is error-prone. Again, synthetic labeled data can be generated to accelerate model development. The synthesis process can ensure high accuracy in the labeling.

Analysts can use the synthetic data models to validate their assumptions and demonstrate the kind of results that can be obtained with their models. In this way the synthetic data can be used in an exploratory manner. Knowing that they have interesting and useful results, the analysts can then go through the more complex process of getting the real data (either raw or de-identified) to build the final versions of their models.

For example, if an analyst is a researcher, they can use their exploratory models on synthetic data to then apply for funding to get access to the real data, which may require a full protocol and multiple levels of approvals. In such an instance, efforts

---

5 Khaled El Emam et al., "A Review of Evidence on Consent Bias in Research," *The American Journal of Bioethics* 13, no. 4 (2013): 42–44.

6 Other governance mechanisms would generally be needed, and we cover these later in the book.

with the synthetic data that do not produce good models or actionable results would still be beneficial, because they will redirect the researchers to try something else, rather than trying to access the real data for a potentially futile analysis.

Another scenario in which synthetic data can be valuable is when the synthetic data is used to train an initial model before the real data is accessible. Then when the analyst gets the real data, they can use the trained model as a starting point for training with the real data. This can significantly expedite the convergence of the real data model (hence reducing compute time) and can potentially result in a more accurate model. This is an example of using synthetic data for transfer learning.

The benefits of synthetic data can be dramatic—it can make impossible projects doable, significantly accelerate AIML initiatives, or result in material improvement in the outcomes of AIML projects.

Synthetic Data as a Proxy

If the utility of the synthetic data is high enough, analysts are able to get results with the synthetic data that are similar to what they would have with the real data. In such a case, the synthetic data plays the role of a proxy for the real data. Increasingly, there are more use cases where this scenario is playing out: as synthesis methods improve over time, this proxy outcome is going to become more common.

We have seen that synthetic data can play a key role in solving a series of practical problems. One of the critical factors for the adoption of data synthesis, however, is trust in the generated data. It has long been recognized that high data utility will be needed for the broad adoption of data synthesis methods.[7] This is the topic we turn to next.

Learning to Trust Synthetic Data

Initial interest in synthetic data started in the early 1990s with proposals to use multiple imputation methods to generate synthetic data. *Imputation* in general is the class of methods used to deal with missing data by using realistic data to replace the missing values. Missing data can occur, for example, in a survey in which some respondents do not complete a questionnaire.

Accurate imputed data requires the analyst to build a model of the phenomenon of interest using the available data and then use that model to estimate what the imputed value should be. To build a valid model the analyst needs to know how the data will eventually be used.

---

7 Jerome P. Reiter, "New Approaches to Data Dissemination: A Glimpse into the Future (?)," *CHANCE* 17, no. 3 (June 2004): 11–15.

With multiple imputation you create multiple imputed values to capture the uncertainty in these estimated values. This results in multiple imputed datasets. There are specific techniques that can be used to combine the analysis that is repeated in each imputed dataset to get a final set of analysis results. This process can work reasonably well if you know in advance how the data will be used.

In the context of using imputation for data synthesis, the real data is augmented with synthetic data using the same type of imputation techniques. In such a case, the real data is used to build an imputation model that is then used to synthesize new data.

The challenge is that if your imputation models are different than the eventual models that will be built with the synthetic data, then the imputed values may not be very reflective of the real values, and this will introduce errors in the data. This risk of building the wrong model has led to historic caution in the application of synthetic data.

More recently, statistical machine learning models have been used for data synthesis. The advantage of these models is that they can capture the distributions and complex relationships among the variables quite well. In effect, they discover the underlying model in the data rather than requiring that model to be prespecified by the analyst. And now with deep learning data synthesis, these models can be quite accurate because they can capture much of the signal in the data—even subtle signals.

Therefore, we are getting closer to the point where the generative models available today produce datasets that are becoming quite good proxies for real data. But there are also ways to assess the utility of synthetic data more objectively.

For example, we can compare the analysis results from synthetic data with the analysis results from the real data. If we do not know what analysis will be performed on the synthetic data, then a range of possible analyses can be tried based on known uses of that data. Or an "all models" evaluation can be performed, in which all possible models are built from the real and synthetic datasets and compared.

Synthetic data can also be used to increase the heterogeneity of a training dataset to result in a more robust AIML model. For example, edge cases in which data does not exist or is difficult to collect can be synthesized and included in the training dataset. In that case, the utility of the synthetic data is measured in the robustness increment to the AIML models.

The US Census Bureau has, at the time of writing, decided to leverage synthetic data for one of the most heavily used public datasets, the 2020 decennial census data. For its tabular data disseminations, it will create a synthetic dataset from the collected individual-level census data and then produce the public tabulations from that synthetic dataset. A mixture of formal and nonformal methods will be used in the synthesis process.[8]

This, arguably, demonstrates the large-scale adoption of data synthesis for one of the most critical and heavily used datasets available today.

Beyond the census, data synthesis is being used in a number of industries, as we illustrate later in this chapter.

Synthetic Data Case Studies

While the technical concepts behind the generation of synthetic data have been around for a few decades, their practical use has picked up only recently. One reason is that this type of data solves some challenging problems that were quite hard to solve before, or solves them in a more cost-effective way. All of these problems pertain to data access: sometimes it is just hard to get access to real data.

This section presents a few application examples from various industries. These examples are not intended to be exhaustive but rather to be illustrative. Also, the same problem may exist in multiple industries (for example, getting realistic data for software testing is a common problem that data synthesis can solve), so the applications of synthetic data to solve that problem will therefore be relevant in these multiple industries. Because we discuss software testing, say, only under one heading does not mean that it would not be relevant in another.

The first industry that we examine is manufacturing and distribution. We then give examples from healthcare, financial services, and transportation. The industry examples span the types of synthetic data we've discussed, from generating structured data from real individual-level and aggregate data, to using simulation engines to generate large volumes of synthetic data.

---

8 Aref N. Dajani et al., "The Modernization of Statistical Disclosure Limitation at the U.S. Census Bureau" (paper presented at the Census Scientific Advisory Committee meeting, Suitland, MD, March 2017).

Manufacturing and Distribution

The use of AIML in industrial robots, coupled with improved sensor technology, is further enabling factory automation for more complex and varied tasks.[9] In the warehouse and on the factory floor, these systems are increasingly able to pick up arbitrary objects off shelves and conveyor belts, and then inspect, manipulate, and move them, as illustrated by the Amazon Picking Challenge.[10]

However, robust training of robots to perform complex tasks in the production line or warehouse can be challenging because of the need to obtain realistic training data covering multiple anticipated scenarios, as well as uncommon ones that are rarely seen in practice but are still plausible. For example, recognizing objects under different lighting conditions, with different textures, and in various positions requires training data that captures the variety and combinations of these situations. It is not trivial to generate such a training dataset.

Let's consider an illustrative example of how data synthesis can be used to train a robot to perform a complex task that requires a large dataset for training. Engineers at NVIDIA were trying to train a robot to play dominoes using a deep learning model (see Figure 1-2). The training needed a large number of heterogeneous images that capture the spectrum of situations that a robot may encounter in practice. Such a training dataset did not exist, and it would have been cost-prohibitive and very time-consuming to manually create these images.

9 Jonathan Tilley, "Automation, Robotics, and the Factory of the Future," McKinsey, September 2017. *https://oreil.ly/L27Ol*.

10 Lori Cameron, "Deep Learning: Our No. 1 Tech Trend for 2018 Is Set to Revolutionize Industrial Robotics," IEEE Computer Society, accessed July 28, 2019. *https://oreil.ly/dKcF7*.

Figure 1-2. The dominoes-playing robot (https://bit.ly/2YXFbwE)

The NVIDIA team used a graphics-rendering engine from its gaming platform to create images of dominoes in different positions, with different textures, and under different lighting conditions (see Figure 1-3).[11] No one actually manually set up dominoes and took pictures of them to train the model—the images that were created for training were simulated by the engine.

---

11 Rev Lebaredian, "Synthetic Data Will Drive Next Wave of Business Applications" (lecture, GTC Silicon Valley, 2019). *https://bit.ly/2yUefyl.*

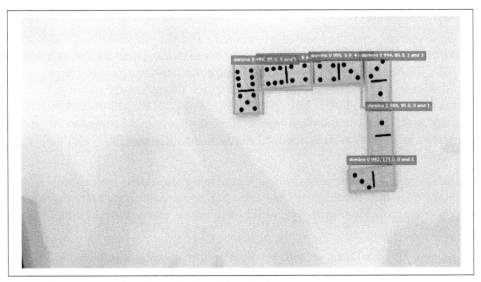

Figure 1-3. An example of a synthesized domino image

In this case the image data did not exist, and creating a large enough dataset manually would have taken a lot of people a long time—not a very cost-effective option. The team used the simulation engine to create a large number of images to train the robot. This is a good example of how synthetic data can be used to train a robot to recognize, pick up, and manipulate objects in a heterogeneous environment—the same type of model building that would be needed for industrial robots.

Healthcare

Getting access to data for building AIML models in the health industry is often difficult because of privacy regulations or because the data collection can be expensive. Health data is considered sensitive in many data-protection regimes, and its use and disclosure for analytics purposes must meet a number of conditions. These conditions can be nontrivial to put in place (e.g., by providing patients access to their own data, creating strong security controls around the retention and processing of the data, and training staff).[12] Also, the collection of health data for specific studies or analyses can be quite expensive. For instance, the collection of data from multiple sites in clinical trials is costly.

The following examples illustrate how synthetic data has solved the data-access challenge in the health industry.

---

12 Mike Hintze and Khaled El Emam, "Comparing the Benefits of Pseudonymisation and Anonymisation under the GDPR," *Journal of Data Protection and Privacy* 2, no. 1 (December 2018): 145–58.

Data for cancer research

There are strong currents pushing governments and the pharmaceutical industry to make their health data more broadly available for secondary analysis. This is intended to solve the data-access problem and encourage more innovative research to understand diseases and find treatments. Regulators have also required companies to make health data more broadly available. A good example of this is the European Medicines Agency, which has required pharmaceutical companies to make the information that they submitted for their drug approval decisions publicly available.[13] Health Canada has also recently done so.[14]

Medical journals are also now strongly encouraging researchers who publish articles to make their data publicly available for other researchers to replicate the studies, which could possibly lead to innovative analyses on that same data (*https://bit.ly/ 2KHfHfz*).

In general, when that data contains personal information, it needs to be de-identified or made nonpersonal before it is made public (unless consent is obtained from the affected individuals beforehand, which is not the case here). However, in practice it is difficult to de-identify complex data for a public release.[15] There are a number of reasons for this:

- Public data has few controls on it (e.g., the data users do not need to agree to terms of use and do not need to reveal their identities, which makes it difficult to ensure that they are handling it securely). Therefore, the level of data transformations needed to ensure that the risk of re-identification is low can be extensive, which ensures that data utility has degraded significantly.

- Re-identification attacks on public data are getting more attention by the media and regulators, and they are also getting more sophisticated. As a consequence, de-identification methods need to err on the conservative side, which further erodes data utility.

- The complexity of datasets that need to be shared further amplifies the data utility problems because a lot of the information in the data would need to be transformed to manage the re-identification risk.

---

13 European Medicines Agency, "External Guidance on the Implementation of the European Medicines Agency Policy on the Publication of Clinical Data for Medicinal Products for Human Use," September 2017. *https:// oreil.ly/uVOna*.

14 Health Canada, "Guidance Document on Public Release of Clinical Information," April 1, 2019. *https://bit.ly/ 33JzHnY*.

15 Khaled El Emam, "A De-identification Protocol for Open Data," IAPP Privacy Tech, May 16, 2016. *https:// bit.ly/33AetZq*.

Synthetic data makes it feasible to have complex open data. Complexity here means that the data has many variables and tables, with many transactions per individual. For example, data from an oncology electronic medical record would be considered complex. It would have information about, for instance, the patient, visits, treatments, drugs prescribed and administered, and laboratory tests.

Synthesis can simultaneously address the privacy problem and provide data that is of higher utility than the incumbent alternative. A good example of this is the synthetic cancer registry data that has been made publicly available by Public Health England (*https://bit.ly/2P5VAL0*). This synthetic cancer dataset is available for download and can be used to generate and test hypotheses, and to do cost-effective and rapid feasibility evaluations for future cancer studies.

Beyond data for research, there is a digital revolution (slowly) happening in medicine.[16] For example, the large amounts of health data that exist with providers and payers contain many insights that can be detected by the more powerful AIML techniques. New digital medical devices are adding more continuous data about patient health and behavior. Patient-reported outcome data provides assessments of function, quality of life, and pain. And of course genomic and other -omic data is at the core of personalized medicine. All this data needs to be integrated into and used for point-of-care and at-home decisions and treatments. Innovations in AIML can be a facilitator of that.

In the next section we examine how digital health and health technology companies can use synthetic data to tap into this innovation ecosystem. And note that more traditional drug and device companies are becoming digital health companies.

Evaluating innovative digital health technologies

Health technology companies are constantly looking for data-driven innovations coming from the outside. These can be innovations from start-up companies or from academic institutions. Typical examples include data analysis (statistical machine learning or deep learning models and tools), data wrangling (such as data standardization and harmonization tools, and data cleansing tools), and data type detection tools (that find out where different types of data exist in the organization).

Because adopting new technologies takes resources and has opportunity costs, the decision to do so must be made somewhat carefully. These companies need a mechanism to evaluate these innovations in an efficient way to determine which ones really work in practice, and, more importantly, which ones will work with their data. The

---

16 Neal Batra, Steve Davis, and David Betts, "The Future of Health," Deloitte Insights, April 30, 2019. *https://oreil.ly/4v_nY*.

best way to do that is to give these innovators some data and have them demonstrate their wares on that data.

Some large companies get approached by innovators at a significant pace—sometimes multiple parts of an organization are approached at the same time. The pitches are compelling, and the potential benefits to their business can be significant. The large companies want to bring these innovations into their organizations. But experience has told them that, for instance, some of the start-ups are pitching ideas rather than mature products, and the academics are describing solutions that worked only on small problems or in situations unlike the companies'. There is a need to test these innovations on their own problems and data.

In the pharmaceutical industry, it can be complex to provide data to external parties because much of the relevant data pertains to patients or healthcare providers. The processes that would be needed to share that data would usually include extensive contracting and an audit of the security practices at the data recipient. Just these two tasks could take quite some time and investment.

Sometimes the pharmaceutical company is unable to share its data externally because of this complexity or because of internal policies, and in that case it asks the innovator to come in and install the software in its environment (see "Rapid Technology Evaluation" for an example). This creates significant complexity and delays because now the company needs to audit the software, address compatibility issues, and figure out integration points. This makes technology evaluations quite expensive and uses up a lot of internal resources. Plus, this is not scalable to the (potentially) hundreds of innovations that the company would want to test every year.

These companies have started to do two things to make this process more efficient and to enable them to bring innovations in. First, they have a standard set of synthetic datasets that are representative of their patient or provider data. For example, a pharmaceutical company would have a set of synthetic clinical trial datasets in various therapeutic areas. These datasets can be readily shared with innovators for pilots or quick proof-of-concept projects.

Rapid Technology Evaluation

Cambridge Semantics (CS), a Boston company developing a graph database and various analytics tools on top of that, was planning to do a pilot with a large prospect in the health space to demonstrate how its tools can be used to harmonize pooled clinical trial data. To do this pilot, it needed to get data from the prospect. That way CS could demonstrate that its tools worked on real data that was relevant for the prospect —there are few things more compelling than seeing a problem solved in an elegant way on your own data.

The initial challenge was that to get data from the prospect, CS would need to go through an audit to ensure that it had adequate security and privacy practices to handle personal health information. That process would have taken three to four months to complete.

An alternative that was considered was for CS to install its software on the prospect's private cloud and then run it there using real data. However, the complexities of introducing new software into a regulated computing environment are not trivial. Furthermore, giving CS staff access to the internal computing environment would have required additional checks and processes. This also would have taken three to four months.

The team landed on a synthetic data solution whereby a number of synthetic datasets were created and given to CS to demonstrate how it would solve the specific problem. The pilot was completed in a few days.

The second process that is used is competitions. The basic idea is to define a problem that needs to be solved and then invite a number of innovators to solve that problem, using synthetic data to demonstrate their solutions. These can be open or closed competitions. With the former, any start-up, individual, or institution can participate, such as by organizing public hackathons or datathons. With the latter, closed competitions, specific innovators are invited to participate.

With public hackathons or datathons, entrants are invited to solve a given problem with a prize at the end for the winning individual or team. The main difference between such public events and the competitions described previously is that the innovators are not selected in advance; rather, participation tends to be more open. The diversity in these competitions means that many new ideas are generated and evaluated in a relatively short period of time. Synthetic data can be a key enabler under these circumstances by providing datasets that the entrants can access with minimal constraints.

A good example of an open competition is the Heritage Health Prize (HHP) (*https://www.kaggle.com/c/hhp*). The HHP was notable for the size of the prize and the size of the dataset that was made available to entrants. At the time of the competition, which lasted from 2011 to 2013, the availability of synthetic data was limited, and therefore a de-identified dataset was created.[17] Because of the challenges of de-identifying open datasets that were noted earlier, it has been more common for health-related competitions to be closed. However, at this point in time there is no compelling reason to

---

17 Khaled El Emam et al., "De-identification Methods for Open Health Data: The Case of the Heritage Health Prize Claims Dataset," *Journal of Medical Internet Research* 14, no. 1 (February 2012): e33. *https://www.jmir.org/2012/1/e33*.

maintain that restriction. Synthetic data is now being used to enable such competitions as described in "Datathons Enabled by Synthetic Data."

In practice, only a small percentage of those evaluations succeed when given a realistic dataset to work with. The innovators that make it through the evaluation or competition are then invited to go through the more involved process to get access to real data and do more detailed demonstrations, or the company may decide to license the innovation at that point. But at least the more costly investments in the technology evaluation or adoption are performed only on candidates that are known to have an innovation that works.

Datathons Enabled by Synthetic Data

The Vivli-Microsoft Data Challenge (*https://bit.ly/2Z5QlhZ*) was held in June 2019 in Boston. The goal of the competition was to propose innovative methods to facilitate the sharing of rare disease datasets, in a manner that maintains the analytic value of the data while safeguarding participant privacy. Rare disease datasets are particularly difficult to share while maintaining participant privacy because they often contain relatively few individuals, and individuals may be identified using only a handful of attributes.

This event gathered 60 participants on 11 teams from universities, hospitals, and pharmaceutical, biotech, and software companies. Each team had five hours to plan and propose a solution, then five minutes to present the solution to the judges. The solutions combined new and existing technologies in interesting ways that were tailored for use in rare disease datasets. Unsurprisingly, the winning team proposed a solution built around the use of synthetic data.

Synthetic data was critical to this event's success as it allowed all participants to "get their hands dirty" with realistic clinical trial data, without needing to use costly secure computational environments or other control mechanisms. The synthetic data grounded the competition in reality by providing participants with example data that their solutions would need to be able to accommodate. Groups that built demos of their solutions were also able to apply their methods to the synthetic data as a proof of concept.

Data challenges like this depend on providing high-quality data to participants, and synthetic data is a practical means to do so.

Another large consumer of synthetic data is the financial services industry. Part of the reason is that this industry has been an early user of AIML technology and data-driven decision making, such as in fraud detection, claims processing, and consumer marketing. In this next section we examine specific use cases in which synthetic data has been applied in this sector.

Financial Services

Getting access to large volumes of historical market data in the financial services industry can be expensive. This type of data is needed, for example, for building models to drive trading decisions and for software testing. Also, using consumer financial transaction data for model building, say, in the context of marketing retail banking services, is not always easy because that requires the sharing of personal financial information with internal and external data analysts.

The following use cases illustrate how synthetic data has been used to solve some of these challenges.

Synthetic data benchmarks

When selecting software and hardware to process large volumes of data, financial services companies need to evaluate vendors and solutions in the market. Instead of having each company evaluate technologies from innovative vendors and academics one by one, it is common to create standardized data benchmarks.

A data benchmark would consist of a dataset and a set of tests that would be performed on that dataset. Vendors and academics can then use their software and hardware to produce the outputs using these data as inputs, and they can all be compared in a consistent manner. Creating a benchmark would make the most sense in situations where the market is large enough and the community can agree on a benchmark that is representative.

In competitive scenarios where multiple vendors and academics can supply solutions to the same set of problems, the benchmarks must be constructed in a manner that ensures that no one can easily game the system. With a standard input dataset, the solutions can just be trained or configured to produce the correct output without performing the necessary analytic computations.

Synthetic data benchmarks are produced from the same underlying model, but each vendor or academic gets a unique and specific set of synthetic data generated from that model. In that way, each entity running the benchmark will need to produce different results to score well on the benchmark.

An example is the STAC-A2 benchmark (*https://www.stacresearch.com/a2*) for evaluating software and hardware used to model financial market risk. The benchmark has a number of quality measures in the output that are assessed during the computation of option price sensitivities for multiple assets using Monte Carlo simulation. There is also a series of performance/scaling tests that are performed using the data.

When financial services companies wish to select a technology vendor, they can compare the solutions on the market using a consistent benchmark that was executed on comparable data. This provides a neutral assessment of the strengths and weaknesses of available offerings without the companies having to perform their own evaluations (which can be expensive and time-consuming) or relying on vendor-specific assessments (which may be biased toward that vendor).

Software testing

Software testing is a classic use case for synthetic data. This includes functional and performance testing of software applications by the software developers. In some cases large datasets are needed to benchmark software applications to ensure that they can perform at certain throughputs or with certain volumes. Extensions of the testing use case are datasets for running software demos by a sales team, and for training users of software on realistic data.

Software testing is common across many industries, and the problems being addressed with synthetic data will be the same. In the financial services sector there are two common use cases. The first is to test internal software applications (e.g., fraud detection) to ensure that they perform the intended functions and do not have bugs. For this testing, realistic input data is needed, and this includes data covering edge cases or unusual combinations of inputs. The second is to test that these applications can scale their performance (for example, response times in automated trading applications are important) to handle the large volumes of data that are likely to be met in practice. This testing must also simulate unusual situations—for example, when trading volumes spike due to an external political or environmental event.

In most software engineering groups, it is not easy to obtain production data. This may be because of privacy concerns or because the data contains confidential business information. Therefore, there is reluctance to make that data available to a large group of software developers. The same applies to making data available for demos and for training purposes. Furthermore, in some cases the software is new and there is insufficient customer data to use for testing.

One alternative that has been used is to de-identify the production data before making it available to the test teams. Because the need for test data is continuous, the de-identification must also be performed on a continuous basis. The cost-effectiveness of continuous de-identification versus that of synthetic data would have to be considered. However, a more fundamental issue is the level of controls that would need to be in place for the software developers to work with the de-identified data. As will be noted later on, re-identification risk is managed by a mix of data transformation and security and privacy controls. Software development groups are accustomed to working with lower levels of these controls.

The data utility demands for software testing are not as high as they are for some of the other use cases that we have looked at. It is possible to generate synthetic data from theoretical distributions and then use them for testing. Another approach that has been applied is to use public datasets (open data) and replicate those multiple times to create larger test datasets or resample with replacement (draw samples from the dataset so that each record can be drawn more than once).

There are more principled methods for the generation of synthetic data for testing, demos, and training. These involve the generation of synthetic data from real data using the same approaches that are used to generate data for building and testing AIML models. This will ensure that the data is realistic and has correct statistical characteristics (e.g., a rare event in the real data will also be a rare event in the synthetic data), and that these properties are maintained if large synthetic datasets are generated.

The next industry that we will consider is transportation. Under that heading we will consider data synthesis for planning purposes through microsimulation models and data synthesis for training models in autonomous vehicles.

Transportation

The use of synthetic data in the transportation industry goes back a few decades. The main driver is the need to make very specific planning and policy decisions about infrastructure in a data-limited environment. Hence the use of microsimulation models became important to inform decision making. This is the first example we consider. The second example is the use of gaming engines to synthesize virtual environments that are used to train AIML models, which are then embedded in the autonomous vehicles.

Microsimulation models

Microsimulation environments allow users to do "what-if" analyses and run novel scenarios. These simulation environments become attractive when there is no real data available at all, and therefore synthetic data needs to be created.

In the area of transportation planning it is, for example, necessary to evaluate the impact of planned new infrastructure, such as a new bridge or a new mall. Activity-based travel demand models can use synthetic data to allow planners to do that.

A commonly used approach to creating synthetic data for these models combines aggregate summaries—for example, from the census, with sample individual-level data that is collected from surveys. Census data would normally provide information like household composition, income, and number of children. The aggregate data would normally cover the whole population of interest but may not have all the needed variables and not to the level of granularity that is desired. The survey data will cover a sample of the population but have very detailed and extensive variables.

Synthetic reconstruction then uses an iterative process such as iterative proportional fitting (IPF) to create synthetic individual-level data that plausibly generates the aggregate summaries and uses the sample data as the seed. The IPF procedure was developed some time ago and has more recently been applied to the data synthesis problem.[18,19] IPF has some known disadvantages in the context of synthesis—for example, when the survey data does not cover rare situations. More robust techniques, such as combinatorial optimization, have been developed to address them.[20]

The next step is to use other data, also collected through surveys or directly from individuals' cell phones, characterizing their behaviors and movements. This data is used to build models, such as the factors that influence an individual's choice of mode of transportation.

By combining the synthetic data with the models, one can run microsimulations of what would happen under different scenarios. Note that the models can be cascaded in the simulation describing a series of complex behaviors and outcomes. For example, the models can inform decisions concerning the impact on traffic, public transportation usage, bicycle trips, and car usage caused by the construction of a new bridge or a new mall in a particular location. These microsimulators can be validated to some extent by ensuring that they give outputs that are consistent with reality under known historical scenarios. But they can also be used to simulate novel scenarios to inform planning and policy making.

Let's now consider a very different use case for synthetic data in the context of developing AIML models for autonomous vehicles. Some of these models need to make decisions in real time and can have significant safety impacts. Therefore, the robustness of their training is critical.

Data synthesis for autonomous vehicles

One of the key functions on an autonomous vehicle is object identification (*https://oreil.ly/GSP7v*). This means that the analysis of sensor data needs to recognize the objects in the vehicle's path and surroundings. Cameras, lidar systems, and radar systems provide the data feeds to support object identification, as well as speed and distance determination of these objects.

Synthetic data is essential to train the AIML models that process some of these signals. Real-world data cannot capture every edge case, or rare or dangerous scenario—such as an animal darting into the vehicle's path or direct sunlight shining into a

---

18 W. Edwards Deming and Frederick F. Stephan, "On a Least Squares Adjustment of a Sampled Frequency Table When the Expected Marginal Totals Are Known," *Annals of Mathematical Statistics* 11, no. 4 (1940): 427–44.

19 Richard J. Beckman, Keith A. Baggerly, and Michael D. McKay, "Creating Synthetic Baseline Populations," *Transportation Research Part A* 30, no. 6 (1996): 415–29.

20 Zengyi Huang and Paul Williamson, "A Comparison of Synthetic Reconstruction and Combinatorial Optimization Approaches to the Creation of Small-Area Micro Data" (working paper, University of Liverpool, 2002); Justin Ryan, Hannah Maoh, and Pavlos Kanaroglou, "Population Synthesis: Comparing the Major Techniques Using a Small, Complete Population of Firms," *Geographical Analysis* 41 (2009): 181–203.

---

camera sensor—that an autonomous vehicle could encounter. Additionally, the captured environment is fixed and cannot respond to changes in the system's behavior when it is run through the scenario multiple times.

The only way to address these gaps is to leverage synthetic data. By generating customizable scenarios, engineers can model real-world environments—and create entirely new ones—that can change and respond to different behaviors. While real-world tests provide a valuable tool for validation, they are not nearly exhaustive enough to prove that a vehicle is capable of driving without a human at the wheel.

The synthetic data used in simulation is generated using gaming technology from video games or other virtual worlds. First, the environment must be created. It can either replicate a location in the real world, like New York City, using actual data, or be an entirely synthetic place. In either case, everything in the environment must accurately simulate the same material properties as the real world—for example, the reflection of light off of metal or the surface of asphalt.

This level of fidelity makes it possible to accurately re-create how a car sees the environment it is driving in, simulating the output from camera, radar, and lidar sensors. The processors on the car then receive the data as if it is coming from a real-world driving environment, make decisions, and send vehicle control commands back to the simulator. This closed-loop process enables bit-accurate, timing-accurate hardware-in-the-loop testing. It also enables testing of the functions of the vehicle under very realistic conditions.

Of course, the computing capacity needed to perform hardware-in-the-loop testing can be quite significant: achieving the fidelity necessary for autonomous vehicle validation is incredibly compute-intensive. First, a detailed world has to be generated. Then the sensor output must be simulated in a physically accurate way—which takes time and massive amounts of compute horsepower.

Summary

Over the last few years we have seen the adoption of synthetic data grow in various industries, such as manufacturing, healthcare, transportation, and financial services. Because data-access challenges are not likely to get any easier or go away anytime soon, the applicability of data synthesis to more use cases is expected to grow.

In this chapter we started with an overview of what synthetic data is and discussed its benefits. We then looked at a number of industries where we have seen how synthetic data can be applied in practice to solve data-access problems. Again, a characteristic of these use cases is their heterogeneity and the plethora of problems that synthesis can solve. Ours is not a comprehensive list of industries and applications, but it does highlight what early users are doing and illustrate the potential.

The examples we gave in this chapter cover multiple types of data. Our focus in this book is on structured data. Many of the concepts we will cover, however, are generally applicable to other types of data as well. In the next chapter we cover important implementation considerations, starting with ensuring that data synthesis is aligned with your organization's priorities. This is followed by a description of the synthesis process and deploying synthesis pipelines. We close with programmatic considerations as you scale data synthesis within the enterprise.

CHAPTER 2

Implementing Data Synthesis

The first decision to be made is whether data synthesis is the best approach for providing data access, compared to alternative privacy-enhancing technologies (PETs). To ensure success with implementing synthesis, it must be aligned with an organization's priorities. In this chapter we first present a decision framework that will enable the objective selection of data synthesis and help you decide when it will fit business priorities, compared to alternatives.

Once data synthesis is selected as the appropriate solution, we can consider the implementation process.

There are two key components to the implementation of data synthesis at the enterprise level: the process and the structure. The process consists of the key process steps, and demonstrates how to integrate synthesis into a data pipeline. Structure would typically be operationalized through a Synthesis Center of Excellence[1] that would have dedicated skills and capacity to generate data for the organization and its customers, as well as provide education and consulting on data synthesis to the rest of the organization. This chapter describes the process and structure in some detail to provide guidance and describe the critical success factors.

In practice, there are many possible scenarios where data synthesis capabilities will need to be deployed. For example, there will be large organizations as well as solo practitioners. Therefore, the following descriptions will need to be tailored to accommodate the specific circumstances.

---

1 A Synthesis Center of Excellence is an organizational entity that is responsible for the adoption and sustainability of data synthesis practices and technology within the enterprise.

When to Synthesize

There are many instances in which data synthesis is a better solution to the data-access problem than other methods that can be used. In this section we present a decision framework for choosing among privacy-enhancing technologies (PETs) that can be used to enable data access, including data synthesis.

As we will see, data synthesis is a powerful approach for many situations that optimize business criteria. There will be specific situations where other privacy-enhancing technologies can also work, and we will present these to ensure that the reader selects the best available tools for the task.

Identifiability Spectrum

An important concept that can help unify the thinking around different PETs is the spectrum of identifiability, illustrated in Figure 2-1.

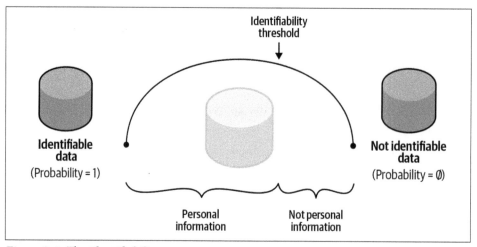

Figure 2-1. The identifiability spectrum

You can think of *identifiability* as being a probability of assigning a correct identity to a record in a dataset. Because it is a probability, it varies from 0 to 1. At one end of this spectrum is perfect identifiability, where the probability of assigning a correct identity to a record is one. At the other end is zero identifiability, where it is impossible to assign an identity to a record correctly.

Zero risk is never really achieved—if your aim is zero risk, then all data will have to be treated as personal information. Therefore, discussions of the "impossibility" of identifying a record or the "irreversibility" of a record's true identity are goals that cannot be attained in practice. In such a case, we are really talking about personal information because zero risk is an impossible standard to meet. Because of that, we will move away from the concept of zero risk and focus on a more pragmatic model.

Any dataset can have a probability of identification along this spectrum (except zero). As you can see in Figure 2-1, along the spectrum there is a threshold value that divides personal information and nonpersonal information or data. When the measured probability in the data is above the threshold, then we have personal information. When the measured probability in the data is at or below the threshold, then we have nonpersonal information.

The PETs that we are interested in place a dataset at a particular point on that spectrum, either above or below the threshold.

This threshold is then also a probability. What should this threshold be? In practice there are a large number of precedents for what this threshold should be in different contexts. We, as a society, have been sharing nonpersonal data for many decades, and there are many examples of organizations around the world that have been setting thresholds and sharing data both publicly and nonpublicly. For example, national statistical agencies such as the Census Bureau in the United States, Statistics Canada in Canada, and the Office of National Statistics in the United Kingdom have been sharing data and using a set of thresholds to do so for a considerable amount of time. And there are others, such as departments of health at the state or provincial levels, large health data custodians, and so on. All this is to say that the choice of a threshold and its interpretation is not very controversial because there are so many precedents that have worked well in practice.

Another key point here is that we are able to measure the probability of identification. There is at least 50 years' worth of literature in statistical disclosure control on this very topic. Any such measurement of risk is based on a model, and models make assumptions; some are very conservative while others can be very permissive.

Just because the probability of identification is measured does not mean that it is done well or in a reasonable way. Some models, for example, are so permissive that they will be very difficult to defend if something goes wrong. Others are so conservative that they will always inflate the risk. The choice of models does matter.

Trade-Offs in Selecting PETs to Enable Data Access

The traditional trade-off when applying any PET was between privacy protection and data utility. This is illustrated in Figure 2-2. The reasoning was that applying PETs would have a negative impact on data utility because PETs imply that the data is transformed. More transformations to the data means that data quality is being gradually reduced. If you wanted a higher level of privacy, then you would pay for this by having a lower level of utility.

Maximum utility would be the original data without any transformations or controls. But the original data, assuming that it is personal information, will have the minimum amount of privacy. Similarly, maximum privacy is attained when the data is not used or disclosed, which is the minimal utility. Both of these extremes are undesirable.

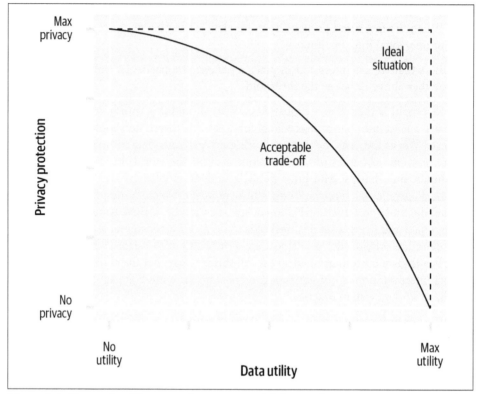

Figure 2-2. The trade-off between data privacy and data utility

Therefore, PETs needed to solve an optimization problem by finding the best point on that curve that would achieve a balance between data privacy and data utility, as illustrated in Figure 2-3. Good privacy-enhancing technology solutions would find a point somewhere along the midpoint on that curve that would simultaneously be below the threshold and result in good data utility. The choice of technology was therefore very important to ensure that an organization was operating as close to the threshold as possible to maximize data utility.

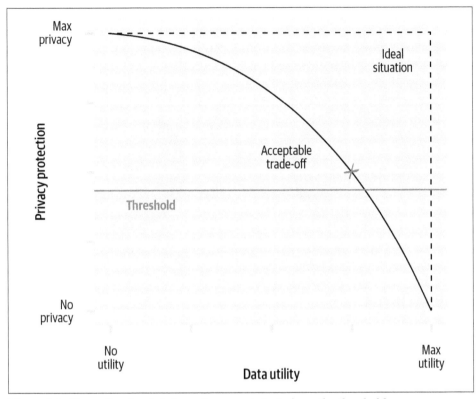

Figure 2-3. The optimal point along the curve is just above the threshold

In addition to data transformations, various controls are sometimes required from the data processors (see Figure 2-4). Controls would be a series of security and privacy practices that are used to manage the overall risk. Therefore, the probability of identification was a function of both data transformations and the controls put into place. Various models were developed to simultaneously assess the risk from the data and the controls.

The advantage of this approach is that you do not need as many data transformations. Because there is a second lever to manage risks, putting in place security and privacy controls was another way to move to a lower probability on that identifiability spectrum. This allows an organization to get closer to the threshold and maximize data utility. So what we have effectively done here is move the line so that at the same level of privacy protection, a higher level of data utility can be achieved.

In general, regulators in many jurisdictions have been open to the concept of managing risk through a combination of data transformations and controls. However, the acceptance has not been universal because there is still some doubt that organizations will truly implement the controls required and maintain them. And that is a big challenge—maintaining trust. Being able to use controls as a mechanism to manage identifiability works in practice only if there is a high level of trust and/or if there is a reliable audit process to ensure that these controls are really in place. Regarding the former, we are on shaky ground, and regarding the latter, it has an impact on the economics of applying a particular approach.

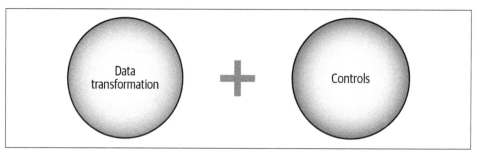

Figure 2-4. Data transformations and controls are sometimes proposed to ensure that the identifiability risk is below the threshold

Decision Criteria

Practically speaking, organizations do not make decisions about which PETs to deploy based only on the balance between data privacy and data utility. There are typically four main factors that are taken into account, as illustrated in Figure 2-5:

- The extent of *privacy protection* (and the extent to which that is compliant with contemporary regulations). This comes down to whether the threshold is acceptable and if the measured risk is below the threshold.

- The extent to which the *data utility* achieves the business objectives. Maximizing data utility is not a universal objective. For example, nonpersonal data used for software testing may have a lower data utility than a dataset that is used by data scientists to drive innovation around clinical trial recruitment. Therefore, there are different degrees of acceptable data utility. An alternative example could be a company that is required by regulation to make its nonpersonal data available to third parties. Such a company may not want to emphasize data utility because it does not perceive that it would benefit from the data sharing.

- *Cost* is also very important. There are two types of costs. The first is *implementation cost*, which is the cost of implementing the PETs, say through pseudonymization. These costs will vary greatly depending on the vendor. The second type of cost is *operational cost*. This is the cost of maintaining the infrastructure and controls to process the data after it has gone through the PET.

- The final factor is *consumer trust*. This will influence whether the consumers (defined here to mean, for example, customers or patients, or even the general public in the case of a government entity) will want to continue to transact with a particular organization. In a healthcare context, it is known that when patients are concerned about how their information will be used, they adopt privacy-preserving behaviors such as not seeking care, self-treating or self-medicating, or omitting vital details in their interactions with their physicians. There is also some evidence that lack of trust in health IT products is slowing their adoption, despite data that supports the benefits of adopting such technology. According to one recent survey from Kantar (*https://oreil.ly/gkz9A*), the lack of confidence in the privacy and security of health technology platforms has an impact on adoption. Consequently, organizations want to use the best available PETs to ensure that they maintain this public trust.

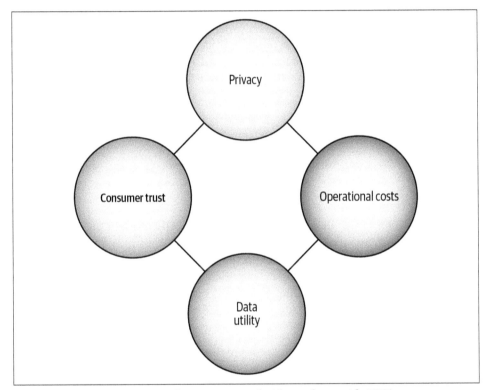

Figure 2-5. Organizations use four criteria to decide on the specific PETs to use

PETs Considered

Let's take a look at the two other PETs and compare them to data synthesis on the data transformations and controls dimensions. More details on secure-multiparty computation can be found in "Secure Multiparty Computation."

Secure Multiparty Computation

Another approach that can be applied to access the data is to use secure multiparty computation. This technology allows computations to be performed on encrypted or garbled data, and it typically involves multiple independent entities that perform the computation collaboratively without sharing or leaking any raw data among themselves. There are multiple ways to do this, such as using what are called secret-sharing techniques (where the data is randomly split among the collaborating entities) or homomorphic encryption techniques (where the data is encrypted and computations are performed on the encrypted values).

In general, to use secure computation techniques the analytics that will be applied need to be known in advance, and the security properties of each analysis protocol must be validated. A good example of this is in public health surveillance where the rate of infections in nursing homes is aggregated without revealing any individual home's rate.[2] This works well in the surveillance case where the analysis is well-defined and static, but setting up secure multiparty computation protocols in practice is complex.

Perhaps more of an issue is that there are few people who understand the secure computation technology and methods underlying many of these techniques, and who can perform these security proofs. This creates key dependencies on very few skilled resources.

Pseudonymization is the first PET we will examine. Organizations that transform only the direct identifiers in their data are using pseudonymization. These direct identifiers are things like names and Social Security numbers, for example. The resulting datasets would have a higher identifiability than any reasonable threshold. Unfortunately, it remains a common (incorrect) belief that pseudonymous information is no longer personal information—that the identifiability is below the threshold.

The HIPAA limited dataset (LDS) also masks only direct identifiers. The LDS allows HIPAA-covered entities to share this pseudonymized data without patient consent (or authorization) for limited purposes such as research, public health, and healthcare operations. The additional control required under the LDS provision is a data-sharing agreement with the data recipient that should ensure, among other things, that the data will not be re-identified, will not be used to contact individuals, and that the obligations will be passed on to subcontractors. Also, because this is still considered personal information, the security provisions under the HIPAA Security Rule would still apply. This means that there is a layer of security controls that must

---

2 Khaled El Emam et al., "Secure Surveillance of Antimicrobial Resistant Organism Colonization in Ontario Long Term Care Homes" *PLoS ONE* 9, no. 4 (2014).

accompany the LDS. The main advantage for an LDS then is avoiding the obligation to obtain consent, but it is not considered to have an identifiability below the threshold.

Under the GDPR, pseudonymous data includes the requirement that additional information that can be used to identify individuals is kept separately and is subject to technical and organizational measures to ensure that it cannot be used in such a way. Also, because pseudonymous data remains personal information, appropriate controls are needed to process the data. The main advantage to using pseudonymization under the GDPR is to reduce the extent of controls required.

Let's consider de-identification. There are a number of different methods that fall under the label of de-identification, which we will discuss.

The HIPAA Safe Harbor method involves removing or generalizing a fixed set of attributes. There are some provisions in Safe Harbor that expand its scope somewhat. For example, one attribute is "any other uniquely identifying number, characteristic or code," which can be interpreted broadly. Also, the covered entity must have no actual knowledge that the remaining information could be used to identify the patient. In practice, these last two items have been applied very lightly, if at all.

It is acknowledged in the disclosure control community that Safe Harbor is not a very strong de-identification standard, and it is not generally recommended. However, for a HIPAA-covered entity, applying that standard provides a straightforward way for that box to be checked and for the data to be declared de-identified. Also, the Safe Harbor standard has been copied in various ways globally. It is attractive because it is very simple to understand and apply. However, strictly speaking, the standard applies only to HIPAA-covered entities and its empirical basis is grounded in analyses performed on US census data. Therefore, the international application of Safe Harbor is questionable.

Risk-based de-identification methods combine statistical methods for measuring the probability of identification and the application of robust controls to further manage the risk of identifiability.

You can see in Figure 2-6 how the three classes of PETs map to the transformation and control dimensions. For example, LDS and GDPR pseudonymization both require data transformations as well as some amount of controls (security, privacy, and/or contractual) to be in place. Fully synthetic data makes minimal demands in terms of controls.

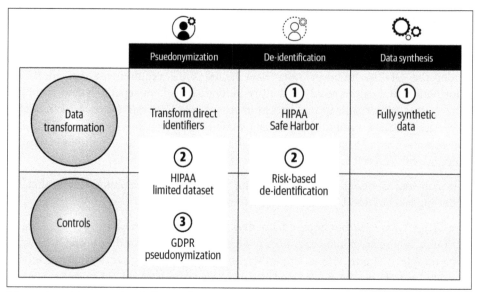

	Psuedonymization	De-identification	Data synthesis
Data transformation	**(1)** Transform direct identifiers	**(1)** HIPAA Safe Harbor	**(1)** Fully synthetic data
	(2) HIPAA limited dataset	**(2)** Risk-based de-identification	
Controls	**(3)** GDPR pseudonymization		

Figure 2-6. Mapping the different classes of PETs on the transformation and control dimensions to see how these trade off

There is of course a trade-off between cost and data utility. For example, implementing a high level of controls entails higher operational costs. This cost becomes more acceptable when the data utility achieved is also high (assuming that data utility is a priority to the organization). Of course, the ideal is when there is low operational cost and high data utility. While this is perhaps a simple view, Figure 2-7 illustrates some important trade-offs that an organization can make.

Higher controls increases the operational cost of a particular PET. More data transformations reduces the data utility. The ideal quadrant is minimal cost and maximum utility, which is the lower left quadrant. The worst quadrant is the top right one, where the operational costs are high and utility is low.

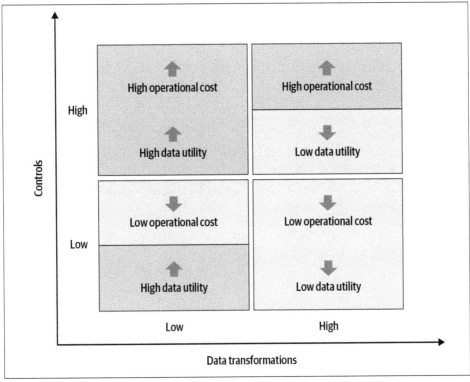

Figure 2-7. The trade-offs between adding controls versus using transformations to manage identifiability

Decision Framework

Figure 2-8 illustrates a model that allows us to select the appropriate PET given the key drivers.

In the first column are the weights assigned to each of the four criteria by the organization. A weight is a value between 0 and 1 to indicate how important a particular criterion is. A higher weight means that it is more important. The weights should reflect an organization's priorities, culture, and risk tolerance.

	Weight	Transform Direct Identifiers	HIPAA LDS	GDPR Pseudonymization	HIPAA Safe Harbor	Risk-Based De-Identification	Data Synthesis
Privacy							
Consumer Trust							
Operational Cost							
Data Utility							
Score (Higher = Better)							

Figure 2-8. The decision framework template for evaluating different PETs

Figure 2-9 contrasts two organizations with very different priorities. On the left is an organization that values privacy protection but is cost-sensitive. In that case, the operational costs will be a factor in its decision making. On the right is an organization that is very focused on utility and that is also very cost-sensitive. In these two examples, trust was scored low. Of course, every organization can make its own trade-offs and can change them over time.

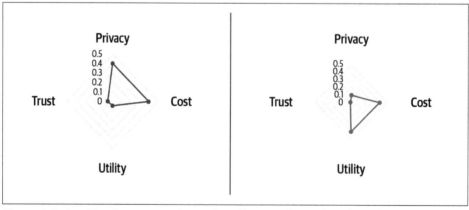

Figure 2-9. A spider diagram can be used to illustrate the trade-offs made by two organizations with differing priorities

The second component of our framework in Figure 2-8 is the rankings. This is the middle part of the table. The rankings would be a number between 1 and 6 for each PET on each of the four criteria. A ranking of 1 means that the PET is better able to meet that criterion. The default rankings that we have been using are shown in Figure 2-10, and our rationale follows.

	Weight	Transform Direct Identifiers	HIPAA LDS	GDPR Pseudonymization	HIPAA Safe Harbor	Risk-Based De-Identification	Data Synthesis
Privacy		6	3	3	5	1	1
Consumer Trust		6	3	3	5	2	1
Operational Cost		1	5	6	2	4	3
Data Utility		1	1	1	4	5	5
Score (Higher = Better)							

Figure 2-10. The decision framework with the rankings included

The transform direct identifier option is assumed to have no controls and are therefore a reflection of some current approaches that are arguably not good practice. The other two types of pseudonymization, HIPAA LDS and GDPR pseudo, do require substantial controls, and under the GDPR additional (all applicable) data is subject to access obligations.

We can see that transforming direct identifiers and HIPAA Safe Harbor have the lowest ranking on privacy because they transform a very small subset of the data and require no additional controls. But they are also the two with the lowest operational costs.

On the trust dimension, data anonymization techniques have been getting negative press recently, and this has eroded consumer trust and raised regulator concerns—hence its ranking. The other methods are not seen as PETs that can guarantee that identifiability is below the threshold.

The score at the bottom is a normalized sum rank, and it is scaled so that a higher value means that it is an option that better matches the priorities of the organization. We can now go through a few examples.

Examples of Applying the Decision Framework

When all of the priorities have the same ranking as in Figure 2-11, we will see that HIPAA Safe Harbor is the least preferred option, with the lowest score. Data synthesis ranks highest because it provides a good balance for the organization across all PETs.

	Weight	Transform Direct Identifiers	HIPAA LDS	GDPR Pseudonymization	HIPAA Safe Harbor	Risk-Based De-Identification	Data Synthesis
Privacy	0.25	6	3	3	5	1	1
Consumer Trust	0.25	6	3	3	5	2	1
Operational Cost	0.25	1	5	6	2	4	3
Data Utility	0.25	1	1	1	4	5	5
Score (Higher = Better)		0.3	0.7	0.5	0	0.7	1

Figure 2-11. A decision example in which the organization has no specific preferences on which criterion to optimize on

By changing the weights we can see which PETs make the most sense under different priorities.

For example, if we have an organization that is very focused on cost minimization and utility maximization at the expense of privacy protection, as in Figure 2-12, just transforming the direct identifiers may be the best option, while methods like HIPAA Safe Harbor are also quite attractive. These will provide very weak privacy assurances and may have an impact on consumer trust. However, these are business priorities that are used today, and with these priorities the simple transformation of direct identifiers is a rational decision.

	Weight	Transform Direct Identifiers	HIPAA LDS	GDPR Pseudonymization	HIPAA Safe Harbor	Risk-Based De-Identification	Data Synthesis
Privacy	0.1	6	3	3	5	1	1
Consumer Trust	0.1	6	3	3	5	2	1
Operational Cost	0.4	1	5	6	2	4	3
Data Utility	0.4	1	1	1	4	5	5
Score (Higher = Better)		1	0.5	0.3	0.3	0	0.3

Figure 2-12. A decision example in which the organization optimizes on cost and utility at the expense of privacy and trust

An organization that puts a lot of weight on trust and privacy, as in Figure 2-13, would select data synthesis as a good solution for data access.

	Weight	Transform Direct Identifiers	HIPAA LDS	GDPR Pseudonymization	HIPAA Safe Harbor	Risk-Based De-Identification	Data Synthesis
Privacy	0.4	6	3	3	5	1	1
Consumer Trust	0.4	6	3	3	5	2	1
Operational Cost	0.1	1	5	6	2	4	3
Data Utility	0.1	1	1	1	4	5	5
Score (Higher = Better)		0	0.6	0.5	0.1	0.8	1

Figure 2-13. A decision example in which the organization optimizes on privacy and trust

Hence, we have a rational way to model and to understand the choices that are being made. Of course, the implication is that when a particular PET is misaligned with an organization's priorities, any attempt to implement the misaligned PET is not going to be successful.

Note that this ranking model is based on certain assumptions. Firstly, we assume that the use cases are applicable. For example, if a form of pseudonymization is found to be a preference, but it is not possible to get consent and no real case can be made for legitimate interests under the GDPR, then pseudonymization will not be a viable option. Therefore, the ranking is applicable only when the PETs are true alternatives for a particular use case. The priority given to data utility is affected by what the organization was accustomed to prior to implementing PETs. For example, if analysts within an organization were historically provided with access to raw data, then they will expect high data utility. If, on the other hand, the analysts were not provided access to any data in the past, then having access to data in any form will be seen as a plus. Therefore, the perception of good enough data utility does depend on history.

Now that we have a method for selecting a PET, and (specifically for our purpose) ensuring that data synthesis is aligned with an organization's priorities and optimizes them, we can examine in more detail the implementation process for data synthesis.

Data Synthesis Projects

Data synthesis projects have some processes that are focused on the generation of synthetic data and the validation of the outputs, and some processes that prepare real data so that it can be synthesized. Validation includes the evaluation of both data utility and privacy assurance. In this section we describe these processes and provide guidance on their application.

Data Synthesis Steps

A general data synthesis process is shown in Figure 2-14. This illustrates the complete process. However, in certain situations and use cases not all of the steps would be needed. We will now go through each of the steps.

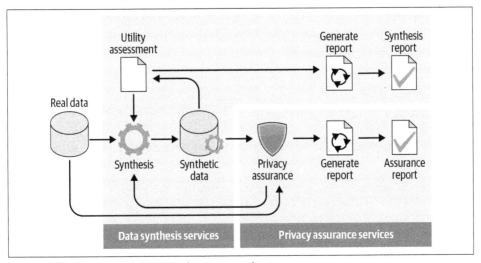

Figure 2-14. The overall data synthesis process[3]

In cases where synthetic data is generated from real data, we need to start from the real data. The real data may be (a) individual-level datasets (or household-level datasets, depending on the context), (b) aggregated data with summaries and cross-tabulations characterizing the population, or (c) a combination of disaggregated and aggregate data. The real data may be open data or nonpublic data coming from a production system, for example.

The synthesis process itself can be performed using different techniques, such as decision trees, deep learning techniques, and iterative proportional fitting. If real data does not exist, then existing models or simulations can be used for data synthesis. The

---

3 Copyright Replica Analytics Ltd. Used with permission.

exact choice will be driven by the specific problem that needs to be solved and the level of data utility that is desired.

In many situations a utility assessment needs to be done. This provides assurance to the data consumers that the data utility is acceptable and helps with building trust in the synthesized data. These utility comparisons can be formalized using various similarity metrics so that they are repeatable and automated.

There are two stages to the utility assessment. The first stage is general-purpose comparisons of parameters calculated from the real and synthetic data—for example, comparisons of distributions and bivariate correlations. These act as a "smoke test" of the synthesis process. The second stage is more workload-aware utility assessments.

Workload-aware utility assessments involve doing analyses on the synthetic data that are similar to the types of analyses that would be performed on the real data if it was available. For example, if the real data would be used to build multivariate prediction models, then utility assessment would examine the relative accuracy of the prediction models built on synthetic datasets.

In cases where the synthetic data pertains to individuals and there are potential privacy concerns, then a privacy assurance assessment should also be performed. Privacy assurance evaluates the extent to which real people can be matched to records in the synthetic data and how easy it would be to learn something new if these matches were correct. There are some frameworks that have been developed to assess this risk empirically.

If the privacy assurance assessment demonstrates that the privacy risks are elevated, then it is necessary to revisit the synthesis process and change some of the parameters. For example, the stopping criterion for training the generative model may need to be adjusted because it was overfit and the synthetic records were quite similar to the real records.

The utility assessment needs to be documented to provide the evidence that the level of utility is acceptable. Data analysts will likely want that utility confidence for the data that they are working on. And for compliance reasons, privacy assurance assessments must also be documented.

In practice, data generation would include utility assessment every time, and therefore they are bundled together as part of the "Data Synthesis Services" component in Figure 2-14. Privacy assurance can be performed across multiple synthesis projects because the results are expected to hold across similar datasets and would apply to the whole generation methodology. Hence that is bundled into a separate "Privacy Assurance Services" component in Figure 2-14.

The activities described previously assume that the input real data is ready to be synthesized. In practice, data preparation will be required before real data can be synthesized. Data preparation is not unique to synthesis projects; however, it is an important step that we need to emphasize.

Data Preparation

When generating synthetic data from real data, as with any data analysis project that starts with real data, there will be a need for data preparation, and this should be accounted for as part of the overall process.

Data preparation includes the following:

- Data cleansing to remove errors in the data * Data standardization to ensure that all of the fields are using consistent coding schemes
- Data harmonization to ensure the data from multiple sources is mapped to the same data dictionary (for example, all the "age" fields in the data, irrespective of the field name and type, are recognized as an "age" field)
- Linking of data from multiple sources—it is not possible to link synthetic data because the generated data does not match real people; therefore, all linking has to happen in advance

With data synthesis, the generated data will reflect any quality challenges of the input data. Data analysis in general requires clean data, and synthesis is a form of analysis; it is easier to cleanse the data before the synthesis process. Messy data can distort the utility assessment process and cause the training of the synthesis models to take longer. Furthermore, as we discuss in the next section with respect to pipelines, data synthesis may happen multiple times for the same real dataset, and therefore it is much easier to have data quality issues addressed *before synthesis*.

Real data will have certain deterministic characteristics, such as structural zeros (these are zero values in the data where it does not make sense for them to be non-zero, i.e., the zero is not a data collection artifact). For example, five-year-olds cannot get pregnant, and therefore the "pregnancy?" value for someone who is five will always be NULL. Also, body mass index (BMI) is a deterministic calculation derived from height and weight. This means that there is no uncertainty in deriving BMI from height and weight. The data synthesis process needs to capture these characteristics and address them. They can be specified a priori either as a series of rules to be satisfied or as edits applied to the synthetic data after the fact. This way the synthesized data will maintain high logical consistency.

A key consideration when implementing data synthesis is how to integrate it within a data architecture or pipeline. In the next section we address this issue and provide some common pipelines.

The Data Synthesis Pipeline

Understanding the data flows that are bringing in data to the data analysts for their AIML projects is important when deciding where data preparation and data synthesis should be implemented in those data flows. It is easiest to explain this through a few examples. All of these examples represent actual situations that we have seen in a variety of industries (such as healthcare and financial services).

One relatively noncomplex setting is where there is a single production dataset or a single data source. In that case the data flows are simple, as illustrated in Figure 2-15. The analysts receiving the synthetic data can then work on that data internally or share it with external parties.

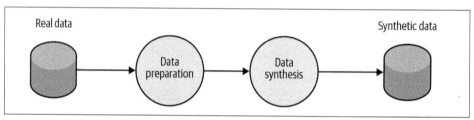

Figure 2-15. Synthesizing data from a production environment

There is a more complex situation in which the data source is in a different organization. For example, the data may be coming from a financial institution to an analytics consultancy or analytics vendor. This is illustrated in the data flows in Figure 2-16.

Under these data flows, the data analysts/data consumers are not performing the data synthesis because they do not have authority or the controls to process the real data (which may be, for example, personally identifying financial information). Under contemporary data protection regulations, such as the GDPR, the obligations and risks to process personally identifying information are not trivial. Therefore, if the data analyst/data consumer can avoid these obligations by having the data supplier or a trusted third party perform the data synthesis, that would be preferable.

There are three common scenarios. Scenario (a) is when the data preparation and data synthesis both happen at the data supplier. In scenario (b) a trusted third party performs both tasks, and in scenario (c) the data supplier performs the data preparation and the trusted third party performs the data synthesis. In this context a trusted third party would be an independent entity that has the authority and controls in place to process the real data.

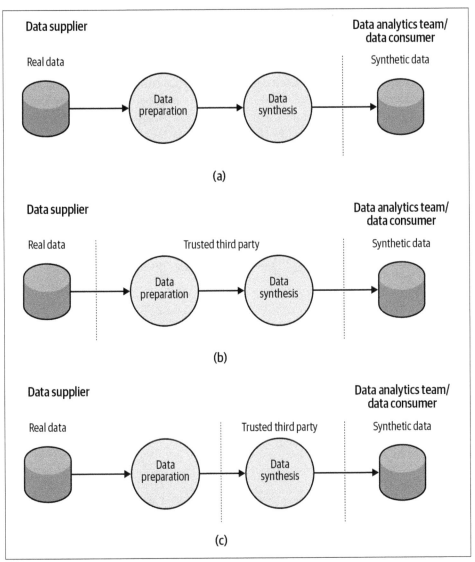

Figure 2-16. Synthesizing data coming from an external data supplier

The last set of examples of data flows that we will look at is where there are many data sources. These are extensions of the examples that we saw in Figure 2-16. In the first data flow shown in Figure 2-17, the data is synthesized at the source by each of multiple data suppliers. For example, the suppliers may be different banks or different pharmacies sending the synthesized data to an analytics company to be pooled and to build models on. Or a medical software developer may be collecting data centrally from all of its deployed customers, with the synthesis performed at the data supplier. Once the synthesized data reaches the data analysts they can build AIML models without the security and privacy obligations of working with real data.

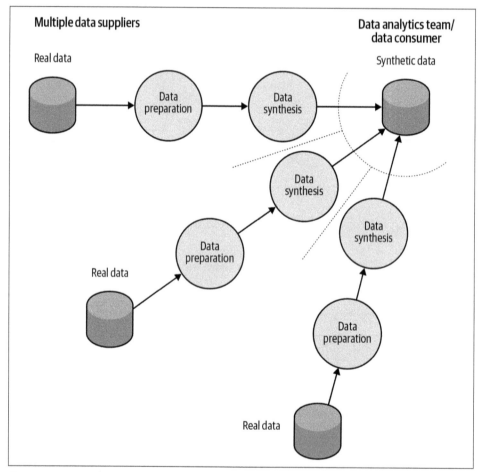

Figure 2-17. Synthesizing data coming from multiple external data suppliers

Another data flow with multiple data sources involves using a trusted third party who prepares and synthesizes the data on behalf of all of them. The synthesis may be performed on each individual data supplier's data, or the data may be pooled first and then the synthesis is performed on the pooled data. The exact setup will depend on the characteristics of the data and the intervals at which the data is arriving at the third party. This is illustrated in Figure 2-18.

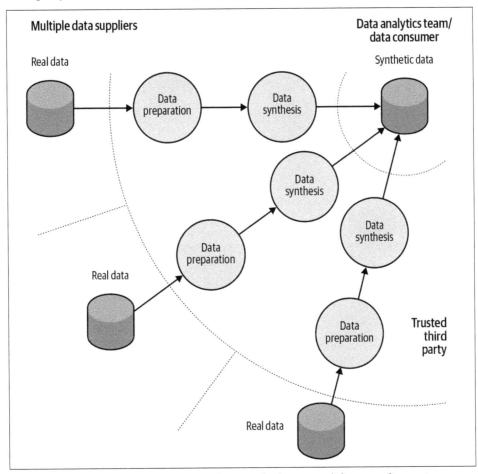

Figure 2-18. Synthesizing data coming from multiple external data suppliers going through a single trusted third party who performs data preparation and synthesis

The final data flow that we will consider, illustrated in Figure 2-19, is a variant of the one we examined earlier in which the data preparation is performed at the source before the data is sent to the trusted third party.

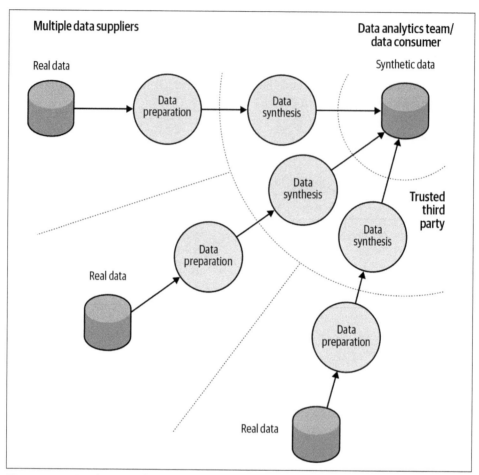

Figure 2-19. Synthesizing data coming from multiple external data suppliers going through a single trusted third party who performs only synthesis

The exact data flow that would be used in a particular situation will depend on a number of factors:

- The number of data sources
- The costs and readiness of the data analyst/data consumer to process real data and meet any regulatory obligations
- The availability of qualified, trusted third parties to perform these tasks
- The ability of data suppliers to implement automated data preparation and data synthesis processes

In large organizations, data synthesis needs to be part of a broader structure that is scalable and that can serve multiple business units and client needs. We present the concept of program management, which supports such scalability, in the next section.

Synthesis Program Management

As data synthesis becomes a core part of an organization's data pipeline, an enterprise-wide structure is needed to ensure that the activities are repeatable and scalable. *Scale* here can mean data synthesis being used by multiple internal business units or as a capability used by multiple clients. This can be supported at a programmatic level by a Center of Excellence (CoE).

A Synthesis CoE is a mechanism that allows an organization to centralize expertise and technology for the generation of synthetic data. In large organizations such centralization is beneficial because it ensures there is learning over time (a shorter feedback loop), methodologies are standardized across projects and datasets, and economies of scale are enabled with respect to the technologies and computational capacity that may be needed.

A CoE can serve a single organization or a consortium of companies operating in the same space. The end users of the synthetic data can be internal, or the CoE can support clients in implementing, say, analytics tools by making appropriate synthetic data available to them.

The skills needed by those operating the CoE span both technical skills, to generate synthetic data and perform privacy assurance, and business analysis skills, to understand user requirements and translate those into synthesis specifications. More importantly, change management is key because transitioning analysts to using synthetic data will require them to provide some education and possibly a series of utility assessments.

CoE for an Analytics Service Provider

ConsultingCo provides management consulting services to a broad spectrum of clients. Some years ago the company created a data analytics business that supports clients by helping them build data analysis capacity (e.g., find, organize, and cleanse the data, and build AIML models to inform the business lines) and doing actual model building for them. One of the big challenges was getting data early on in the process.

At the beginning of these engagements it was often the case that the clients did not have a full accounting of all of their data assets and the quality of that data. There were also questions about the lawful basis for performing secondary analysis on that data. Complicating matters was the internal reluctance by business lines to share data or to invest in making data available for analytics before the value of the analytics was demonstrated.

The data synthesis team at ConsultingCo provides synthetic data early on in these engagements to enable analysts to demonstrate the value of using the data that is available to the clients, and to show how models that can be built would inform business decisions. The synthetic data can be generated without real data or it can be based on small samples of real data.

The ability to demonstrate value at the beginning of the process greatly facilitates getting buy-in for acquiring, cleaning, and using the data within the organization. The synthesis CoE gives ConsultingCo a competitive advantage because the likelihood of success of these engagements increases.

Data synthesis will be a new methodology for many organizations. While the introduction of any data analytics method and technology involves some organizational change, data synthesis introduces some specific considerations during the implementation. In the next section, best practices for the implementation of data synthesis will be discussed to help increase your likelihood of smoothly adopting this approach.

Summary

This chapter provided a decision framework to assess the alignment of data synthesis with an organization's priorities, followed by the workflows and pipelines that can be used for this implementation. We closed with some practical considerations for program management with synthesis implemented at scale. These three components are important from an enterprise implementation perspective.

After getting this far, you should have a high-level implementation road map and some key elements of a business case for synthesizing data to enable access to data. In the next few chapters we will focus more on the methodology and technology of data synthesis.

CHAPTER 3

Getting Started: Distribution Fitting

A straightforward way to think about the process of data synthesis is that we are trying to model both the distributions of the real data and the structure of the real data. Based on that model we can then generate synthetic data that retains the characteristics of the original data. In this chapter we cover the first step in that process—modeling distributions. Once you know how to do that, we'll move on to modeling the structure of the data in Chapter 5.

The starting point of modeling distributions is understanding how to fit individual variables to known distributions (or "classical" distributions, such as the normal and exponential). Once we are able to do that, we can generate data from these distributions that have the same characteristics as the original data.[1]

The next step will be to enable the modeling of nonclassical distributions. Some real-world data or real-world phenomena do not follow a classical distribution. We still want to be able to synthesize data that does not follow classical distributions. Therefore, we outline how machine learning models can be used to fit unconventional data distributions.

---

[1] Chong K. Liew, Uinam J. Choi, and Chung J. Liew, "A Data Distortion by Probability Distribution," *ACM Transactions on Database Systems* 10, no. 3 (September 1985): 395–411.

Framing Data

Any data analysis task begins with a pile of data that needs to be transformed into a data frame. A *data frame* is a table of data in which each row, also known as a *record*, is a complete, self-contained example of the data being represented. Each column, also known as a *variable* or *field*, is a detail about the record. Every field in a column must be of the same data type.

Framing the data can be hard work. Columns must be regimented into the expected data type; errors and exceptions need to be weeded out; relational data must be unfolded into the frame by joins; missing data needs to be estimated, extrapolated, neutralized, or omitted. This requires knowledge about the data that is not in the data, notably knowledge about what to expect. Like my hairdresser, the person who does the data preparation is not going to be replaced by artificial intelligence anytime soon.

Once data has been framed, a substantial arsenal of analytical weaponry developed in the last three hundred years can be deployed to dissect it, from the probabilities of Thomas Bayes to the machine learning guiding the electrons-with-consequences in our increasingly virtual world today. We can use these techniques to model a data frame's distributions and probabilities, forecast future values, measure how much information it contains, estimate the error around any data model we create, and create control strategies for optimizing real-time data in real time. So many exciting things.

But the topic of this book is data synthesis, which brings in a new angle: anonymity. Not only do we need to model the distribution of real data and then create synthetic data that fits it well, but we also have to ensure that the original data cannot be determined from the synthetic data. There will be more on the privacy question later in the book.

Once we have a data frame, we need to understand and model the distribution of the fields within it.

How Data Is Distributed

Individual data variables can have many types and distributions. The following are among the most common:

Unbounded real numbers, potentially ranging from −infinity to +infinity—for example, the Gaussian or normal distribution, which tends to apply when random numbers are added together, as in Figure 3-1.

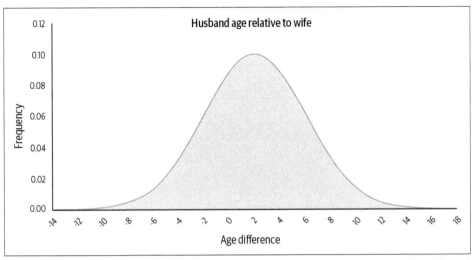

Figure 3-1. Example of a normal distribution for the difference between a husband's and wife's ages

Bounded real numbers with definite upper and lower bounds—for example, Bayesian probabilities ranging from 0 to 1, or, equivalently, 0% to 100%. These are particularly useful for expressing the likelihood of an estimate or confidence level, as in Figure 3-2.

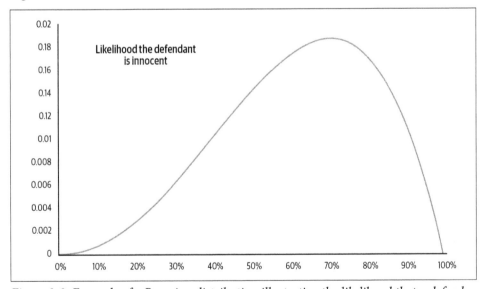

Figure 3-2. Example of a Bayesian distribution illustrating the likelihood that a defendant is innocent

Nonnegative integers—for example, Poisson distributed counts of events, ranging from 0 to *n*, in Figure 3-3.

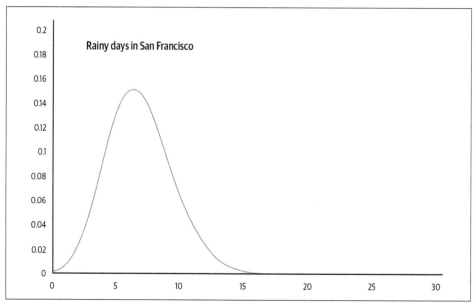

Figure 3-3. Example of a Poisson distribution illustrating the number of rainy days per month in San Francisco

Logarithmic distributions, which may be integers or real numbers and tend to reflect physical systems with multiplicative effects—for example, Benford's distribution of first digits in accounting numbers, as in Figure 3-4.

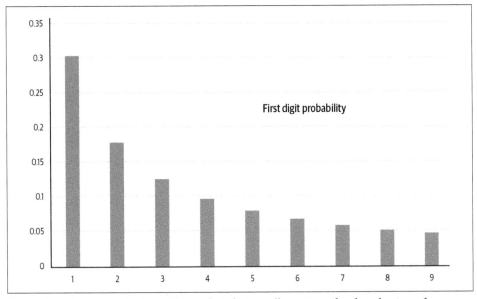

Figure 3-4. Example of a logarithmic distribution illustrating the distribution of accounting numbers

Binomial integers, which model the number of successes from a series of independent experiments—for example, the probability of the number of heads from 10 coin tosses, as in Figure 3-5.

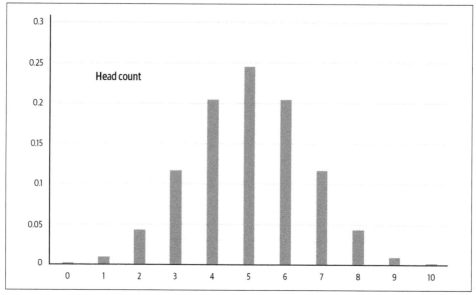

Figure 3-5. Example of a binomial distribution showing the probability of a specific number of heads in 10 coin tosses

Nonclassical distributions based on physical realities—for example, the hospital discharge data in Figure 3-6. This shows the distribution of ages of individuals who were discharged from hospitals in a specific US state.

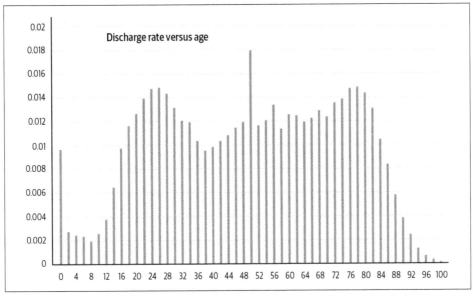

Figure 3-6. The distribution of ages of individuals discharged from a hospital

Factor data, or *category data*, has a definite number of categories, as in Figure 3-7.

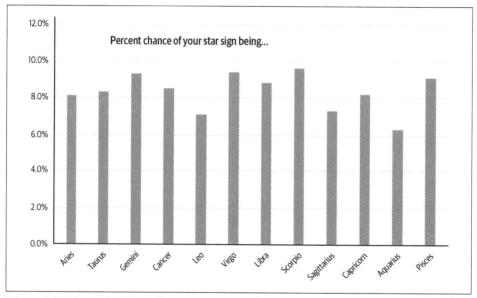

Figure 3-7. The probability of being in a particular astrological sign—an example of a factor distribution

Factor data is a little different from other types of data because a factor's relationship with other factors is not linear:

- It may have sequence: birth, marriage, death events, with the second being optional and not necessarily unique
- It may have quasi-sequence: Sunday, Monday, Tuesday… (peppered with national holidays!)
- It may have no sequence: red, green, blue…

To work with the established analytical techniques, factor data needs to be turned into numbers. The usual approach is to split the factor into multiple variables, one for each factor, containing 1 if it is that factor and 0 if it isn't (this is also called *one-hot encoding*). This approach excludes some analysis techniques such as multivariate regression, due to matrix inversion failure. However, when used with more advanced neural network modeling techniques, it has the advantage that the results are in the range 0 to 1 and represent probability of a particular factor being right.

The challenge with this approach is that when there are many categories, this results in a large number of new variables being added to the dataset. A more efficient alternative is *binary encoding*, in which each factor is encoded into its binary equivalent. For example, if we have five possible values, then the third value is encoded "011."

Time series data contains records of sequential measurements in which the probability distribution for the present record will depend on earlier measurements. In data science courses, the time to the next eruption of the Old Faithful geyser in Yellowstone National Park is a common teaching example, and is illustrated in Figure 3-8.

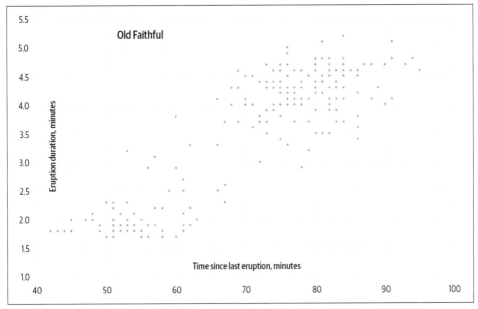

Figure 3-8. Modeling Old Faithful eruptions

Similarly, in financial markets, price changes relative to previous values are quite important. The Dow Jones Industrial Average (DJIA) over the last five years can be seen in Figure 3-9.[2]

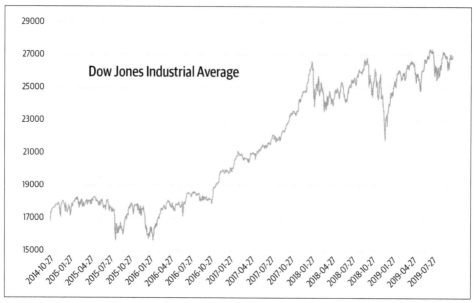

Figure 3-9. Financial market time series

But do we care what the actual stock price is? People are more interested in knowing how much their investment is now relative to when they bought in. That, again, raises questions: What time horizon is relevant? Is the time horizon eroding my data quality? The charts shown in Figures 3-10 and 3-11 show data rebased (or recalculated) from Figure 3-9 as a percentage change over time, and they indicate the data erosion penalty. (And they give a lesson in long-term rather than short-term investing!)

---

2 At the time of the final editing of this book, the market conditions changed dramatically. Therefore, this is only an example reflective of the good old days.

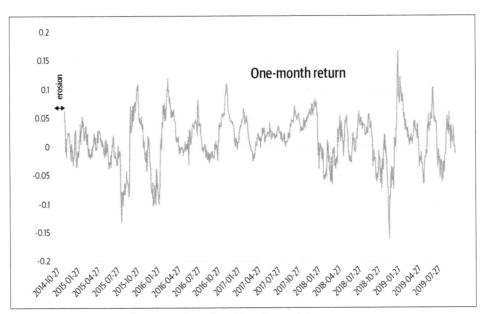

Figure 3-10. One-month returns based on Dow Jones data

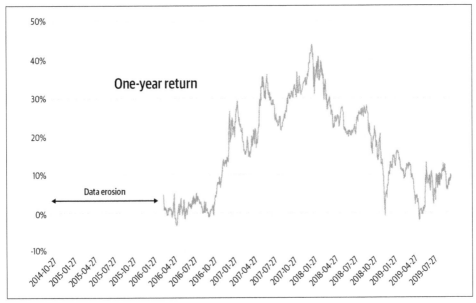

Figure 3-11. One-year returns based on Dow Jones data

Time series data gets worse. Longitudinal data (for example, maintenance records or doctor's visits) is composed of sparse records that are taken at sporadic intervals but that happen in a clear sequence and can be modeled by Markov chains, which is beyond the scope of this chapter.

Finally, unstructured data, such as Twitter feeds or doctor's notes, can really be applied only if they can be structured in some manner—for example, using keywords to create sentiment indicators, which is again beyond the scope of this chapter.

Fitting Distributions to Real Data

Fitting a distribution to individual variables (*univariate distributions*) is, on the surface, fairly straightforward. An error function, such as squared error, can be used to measure how close a distribution is to the real data. Frequency distribution functions are parameterized equations. For example, Gaussian distributions have mean and standard deviation parameters; machine learning models have neural network weights. *Fitting* is searching for the parameters that optimize the error function, and plenty of optimization algorithms exist to help us do that.

Modeling univariate distributions, however, is often not enough. Let's revisit Old Faithful and plot the probability density for each variable along its axis, as in Figure 3-12.

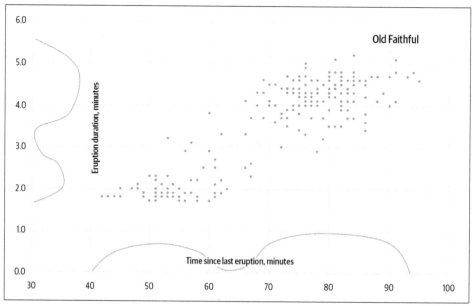

Figure 3-12. Old Faithful data with the probability density along each axis

If we blindly generate synthetic data according to those distributions, the synthesized data will have unintended ellipses of high density, as shown in Figure 3-13.

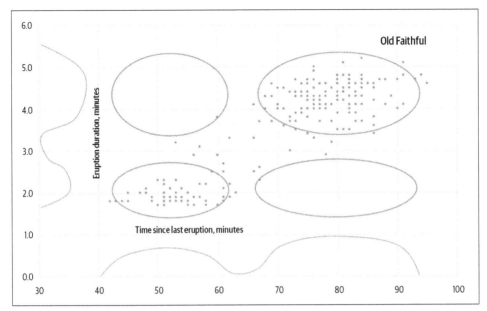

Figure 3-13. Old Faithful data illustrating high-density ellipses

What we really need is a "multivariate" probability, which is a distribution that takes into consideration both variables at once, as in Figure 3-14.

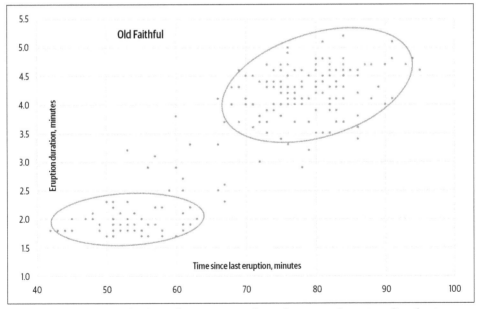

Figure 3-14. Old Faithful data illustrating synthesis from a multivariate distribution

Note that by considering both variables together, we have not only removed the unintended ellipses of high density but also allowed the desired ellipses to rotate.

Generating Synthetic Data from a Distribution

If the fitted distribution is a known or classical one, and the fitting process has determined the distribution parameters, then synthetic data can be generated using Monte Carlo methods. That is, data is just sampled from these distributions.

The brute-force approach to generating synthetic data from nonclassical distributions is straightforward: generate randomized datapoints evenly across the data range, or as probability suggests, and adopt or reject it according to whether it improves the fit to the distribution.

More sophisticated methods exist, such as using histogram equalization to generate distributed synthetic data from uniform random data, but with sufficient computing capacity, it can be easiest to keep it simple.

Measuring How Well Synthetic Data Fits a Distribution

Several measures exist to grade how well a probability distribution fits to a single variable within a dataset, including the Chi-squared measure and the Kolmogorov-Smirnov (KS) test.

KS is particularly robust because it looks at the difference between the cumulative probability and the cumulative data count, which makes it fairly indifferent to the actual distribution of the data. Let's plot the cumulative distribution of the probability (assuming it follows a quadratic distribution) and sample data in Figure 3-6 in Figure 3-15.

The KS measure is essentially the area between the two curves. The smaller the area, the better the fit of the distribution to the data.

Extending the KS approach to multiple dimensions is tricky: it is not easy to define *cumulative* across many variables of different types, with a sparse dataset occupying tiny pockets within the total volume of space. One approach is to use the sparse dataset as a guide to what is important, limiting the measurement to areas where data exists.

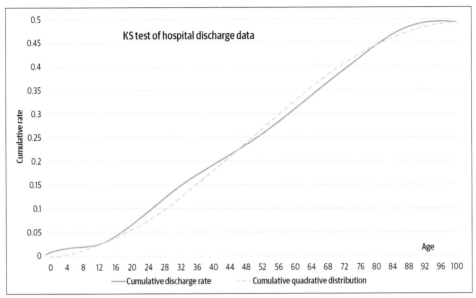

Figure 3-15. KS test of hospital discharge data

The Overfitting Dilemma

Let's take a look at the hospital discharge rate again. The red line in Figure 3-16 is a quadratic fit based on three variables and is a generalization of the 51-datapoint distribution.

Figure 3-16. The hospital discharge data with a best fit standard distribution

We can improve the fit by using models with more variables. For example, a spline might produce something like Figure 3-17.

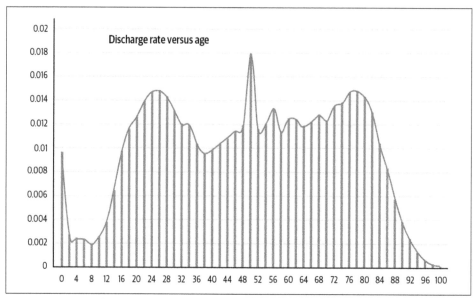

Figure 3-17. Overfitting to a distribution of hospital discharge ages

While this passes through every datapoint, can it be justified? For example, given that we don't have any evidence for there being a sudden peak at 50, should we incorporate it into the model? This is known as the problem of overfitting, where we start to fit to artifacts in a particular dataset, rather than to the actual distribution that the sample represents. We're probably looking for something more like Figure 3-18.

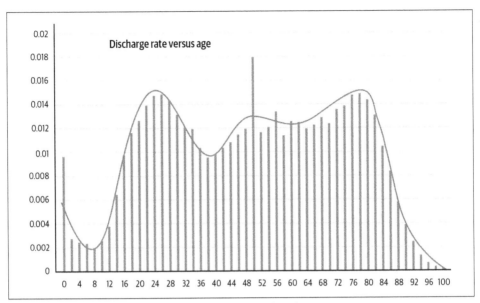

Figure 3-18. Better fit to a hospital discharge age distribution

This issue is widespread and causes many problems. Models that appear to fit well don't perform well when applied to new data because the analyst tried too hard to fit to the old data.

The problem is acute when the intent is to anonymize data by synthesis: overfitting gives away the original data, defeating the object of the exercise.

Solving this problem requires two things. The first is an approach that allows a distribution to start from a neutral point and journey slowly to a closer and closer fit to the data, trading off between simplicity of distribution and goodness of fit at each step. The second is a measure to know when the best trade-off point has been reached.

Most distribution-fitting approaches can find some kind of journey from a neutral start to an overfitted state. A B-tree, for example, can add more and more branches; neural networks can use weight pruning or steepest descent (my favorite for its purity); radial basis functions can add more bases.

A measure to know when the best trade-off point has been reached requires a subsample approach. Let's go back to how we expressed it a few paragraphs ago: models that appear to fit well don't perform well when applied to new data because the analyst tried too hard to fit to the old data. So somehow we need to measure how representative the data is of the distribution from which it comes.

How can we do that without more data to compare it to? We can't, so we do the next best thing: we hold back some of the data (i.e., create a holdout sample, which can be, say, 25% or 33% of the training dataset) and see how well it fits to the distribution created with the rest of the data. What we see is something like Figure 3-19.

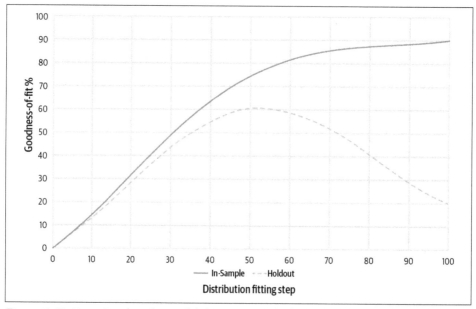

Figure 3-19. Ensuring that the model does not overfit the data

Notice how the goodness of fit to the holdout sample reaches a peak and then, as overfitting starts to happen, drops off, even though the in-sample fit continues to get better. In this example, the optimal fit occurs at 50 steps. The fitting process can then be repeated without the holdout sample, stopping at the 50th step to avoid overfitting and thus finding the optimum trade-off between goodness of fit and the risk of identification.

With small datasets, the process is repeated with multiple holdout samples in order to determine the optimum trade-off point.

A Little Light Weeding

This process allows univariate synthetic data to be generated that retains as much of the underlying structure as possible without capturing so much information that the original data can be identified. However, a synthetic datapoint could be generated that is coincidentally close to one of the original datapoints. Therefore, as a final step, it is worth checking whether this is the case and rejecting any datapoints that are too close.

Summary

In this chapter we first looked at classical distributions and how we can fit real data to them. Many real datasets do not follow classical distributions, and therefore there will be a mismatch between the fitted distributions and the real data. One can use machine learning models to learn the distribution of the data. This allows the modeling of nonclassical distributions that can be multimodal, which can be heavily skewed or have other unusual characteristics. However, when we do that we need to be aware of the risk of overfitting and ensure that we are learning the distribution in a manner that is generalizable to other data.

In the next chapter we will start exploring the second component of data synthesis: modeling the structure of the data. The first step in that process is to look at ways to evaluate data utility. To understand what is a good data structure, we need to be able to define and measure the concept of a good data structure.

CHAPTER 4

Evaluating Synthetic Data Utility

To achieve widespread use and adoption, synthetic data needs to have sufficient utility to produce analysis results similar to the original data's.[1] This is the trust-building exercise that was discussed in Chapter 1. If we know precisely how the synthetic data is going to be used, we can synthesize the data to have high utility for that purpose—for example, if the specific type of statistical analysis or regression model that will be performed on the synthetic data is known. However, in practice, synthesizers will often not know a priori all of the analyses that will be performed with the synthetic data. The synthetic data needs to have high utility for a broad range of possible uses.

This chapter outlines a data utility framework that can be used for synthetic data. A common data utility framework would be beneficial because it would allow for the following:

- Data synthesizers to optimize their generation methods to achieve high data utility

- Different data synthesis approaches to be consistently compared by users choosing among data synthesis methods

- Data users to quickly understand how reliable the results from the synthetic data would be

---

1 Jerome P. Reiter, "New Approaches to Data Dissemination: A Glimpse into the Future (?)," *CHANCE* 17, no. 3 (June 2004): 11–15.

There are three types of approaches to assess the utility of synthetic data that have been used:

- Workload-aware evaluations
- Generic data utility metrics
- Subjective assessments of data utility

Workload-aware metrics look at specific feasible analyses that would be performed on the data and compare the results or specific parameters from the real and the synthetic data.[2] These analyses can vary from simple descriptive statistics to more complex multivariate models. Typically an analysis that was done or was planned on the real data is replicated on the synthetic data.

Generic assessments would consider, for example, the distance between the original and transformed data.[3] These often do not reflect the very specific analysis that will be performed on the data but rather provide broadly useful utility indicators when future analysis plans are unknown. To interpret generic metrics, they need to be bounded (e.g., from 0 to 1), and there should be some accepted yardsticks for deciding whether a value is high enough or too low.

A subjective evaluation would get a large enough number of domain experts who would look at a random mix of real and synthetic records and then attempt to classify each as real or synthetic. If a record looks realistic enough, then it would be classified as real, and if it has unexpected patterns or relationships, then it may be classified as synthetic. For example, for a health dataset, clinicians may be asked to perform the subjective classification. The accuracy of that classification would then be evaluated.

In the next few sections we present a hybrid framework for evaluating the utility of synthetic data by considering some workload-aware metrics as well as some generic metrics covering possible univariate, bivariate, and multivariate models that would be constructed from the data. We do not illustrate a subjective evaluation.

In addition to replicating an analysis performed on a real dataset, our metrics are generic in that exact knowledge of the desired analysis is not required, and they are

---

2 Josep Domingo-Ferrer and Vicenç Torra, "Disclosure Control Methods and Information Loss for Microdata," in *Confidentiality, Disclosure, and Data Access: Theory and Practical Applications for Statistical Agencies*, ed. Pat Doyle et al. (Amsterdam: Elsevier Science, 2001); Kristen LeFevre, David J. DeWitt, and Raghu Ramakrishnan, "Workload-Aware Anonymization," in *Proceedings of the 12th ACM SIGKDD International Conference on Knowledge Discovery and Data Mining* (New York: Association for Computing Machinery, 2006): 277–286.

3 A. F. Karr et al., "A Framework for Evaluating the Utility of Data Altered to Protect Confidentiality," *The American Statistician* 60, no. 3 (2006): 224–32.

---

workload-aware in that they consider many likely simple and complex models that would be developed in practice.

Synthetic Data Utility Framework: Replication of Analysis

We use the census data from the UC Irvine machine learning repository to illustrate the replication of an analysis. This dataset has 48,842 records, with the variables summarized in Figure 4-1.

Variable	Interpretation	Categories
continent_name	Continent of birth	North America, Asia, Europe, South America
marital_status	Marital status	Never-married, Married-civ-spouse, Divorced, Married-spouse-absent, Separated, Married-AF-spouse, Widowed
workclass		State-gov, Self-emp-not-inc, Private, Federal-gov, Local-gov, Self-emp-inc
education	Level of education	HS-grad, Bachelors, Masters, Some-college, Assoc-acdm, Assoc-voc, Doctorate, Prof-school, Preschool, 1st-4th, 5th-6th, 7th-8th, 9th, 10th, 11th, 12th
occupation	Occupation	Adm-clerical, Exec-managerial, Handlers-cleaners, Pro-specialty, Other-service, Sales, Craft-repair, Transport-moving, Farming-fishing, Machine-op-inspct, Tech-support, Protective-serv, Armed-Forces, Priv-house-serv
relationship	Relationship to others in the household	Not-in-family, Husband, Wife, Own-child, Unmarried, Other-relative
race	Race	White, Black, Asian-Pac-Islander, Amer-Indian-Eskimo, Other
sex	Sex	Male, Female
income	Income Category	<=50K, >50K

Variable	Interpretation
age	Age
capital	Capital gain/loss
hours_per_week	Hours the individual worked per week

Figure 4-1. The variables that we use in the census dataset. The top table contains the categorical variables and their valid values, and the bottom table contains the continuous variables.

We built a classification tree to classify the income variable, which has two categories. All of the other variables were used as predictors. This is a typical analysis that is performed on this dataset. The tree-building exercise used 10-fold cross-validation.

The resulting tree on the real dataset is shown in Figure 4-2. The tree built from the synthetic data was exactly the same, and therefore we will not repeat it here.

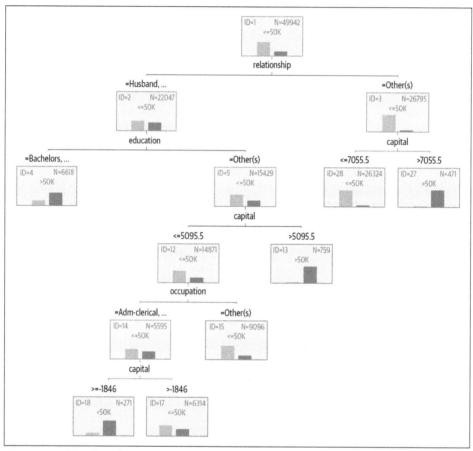

Figure 4-2. The classification tree developed from the census dataset to predict the income class

The first split in the tree is based on the relationship variable. If the relationship is husband or wife, then we go to node number 2; otherwise, we go to node number 3. In node 3 the split is based on capital gains of just over $7,000.00. Therefore, those who are not husbands or wives and have capital gains over $7,055.50 will tend to have an income greater than $50K.

In node 2 there is another split. Here, those husbands or wives who have a bachelor's, a master's, a doctorate, or who went to a professional school also have an income greater than $50K. Otherwise, those with less education go to node 5, which splits on capital again. And so on as we navigate through the tree.

The importance of the variables in the real and synthetic datasets is shown in Figure 4-3. This reflects each variable's contributions to the classification of income. As can be seen, the variable importance is exactly the same in models from both types of datasets.

Real	Synthetic
Capital	Capital
Occupation	Occupation
Education	Education
Age	Age
Relationship	Relationship
Marital status	Marital status
Hours per week	Hours per week
Workclass	Workclass
Sex	Sex

Figure 4-3. The importance of the variables in terms of their contribution to the classification of income

We can see from this replication of analysis that the real and synthetic data generated the same classification tree. That is a meaningful test of whether a synthetic dataset has sufficient utility. If the same results can be obtained from real and synthetic data, then the synthetic data can serve as a proxy.

However, it is not always possible to perform the same analysis as the real data. For example, the original analysis may be very complex or labor-intensive, and it would not be cost-effective to replicate it. Or an analysis on the real dataset may not have been performed on the original data yet; therefore, there is nothing to compare against. In such a case, more general-purpose metrics are needed to evaluate the utility of the data, which is the topic we turn to next.

Synthetic Data Utility Framework: Utility Metrics

Different types of analyses that may be performed on a synthetic dataset and the distinguishability of the synthetic dataset from the original dataset are the basis of our data utility framework. We use the clinical trial datasets described in "Example Clinical Trial Data" to illustrate the various techniques.

To generate each synthetic clinical trial dataset, a model was built from the real data and then the synthetic data was sampled from that model. Specifically, a form of classification and regression tree (CART)[4] called a *conditional inference tree* was used to generate the synthetic data.[5] The main advantage of this method is that it can capture the structure of the data by finding interactions and nonlinear relationships in a data-driven way, addressing variable selection biases and handling missing data in an unbiased manner.

Example Clinical Trial Data

For the illustrations that we use in the remainder of this chapter, we synthesized the data for two oncology clinical trials.

The first trial was an evaluation of a drug that is given post-surgery to patients who have had their gastrointestinal stromal tumors removed. A total of 732 patients participated in the trial, and the primary endpoint was recurrence-free survival. The second trial was a comparison of a novel gemcitabine treatment for inoperable, and potentially metastatic, prostate cancer with standard treatment. A total of 367 patients participated in the second trial. The data was obtained from Project Data Sphere (*https://projectdatasphere.org*), which makes oncology clinical trial data accessible for secondary analysis.

For the purposes of this chapter, we focus on the synthesis of the cross-sectional component of the two datasets. The first trial had 129 variables detailing each patient's demographics, treatment received, and outcomes. The second trial had 88 variables.

---

4 Jerome P. Reiter, "Using CART to Generate Partially Synthetic Public Use Microdata," *Journal of Official Statistics* 21, no. 3 (2005): 441–62.

5 Torsten Hothorn, Kurt Hornik, and Achim Zeileis, "Unbiased Recursive Partitioning: A Conditional Inference Framework," *Journal of Computational and Graphical Statistics* 15, no. 3 (September 2006): 651–74.

Comparing Univariate Distributions

This type of comparison between real and synthetic data indicates whether the variable distributions are similar.

Let's look at the example in Figure 4-4. Here we have the original age variable and the synthesized age variable for one of the clinical trial datasets we have been looking at. The synthesized age distribution is quite similar to the original age distribution, and therefore the data utility here is expected to be high. We do not want the distribution to be exactly the same because that could be an indicator of a privacy problem.

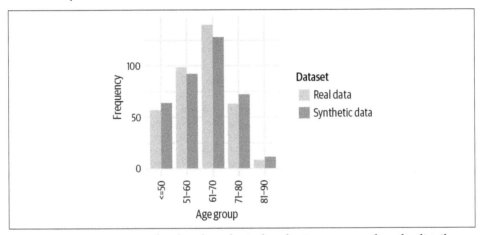

Figure 4-4. A comparison of real and synthetic distributions on age when the distributions are similar

It is informative to look at some examples in which there are differences between the real and synthetic distributions.

When data synthesis methods do not work well (for example, poorly fitted models), we get something like the examples in Figure 4-5 for clinical trial height data and in Figure 4-6 for clinical trial weight data. In these examples you can clearly see the mismatch between the original distributions and the generated distributions. It does not look like the synthesized data took much of the real data into account during the generation process! We don't want that outcome, of course. However, one of the first things to look at in the synthetic data is how well the distributions match the original data.

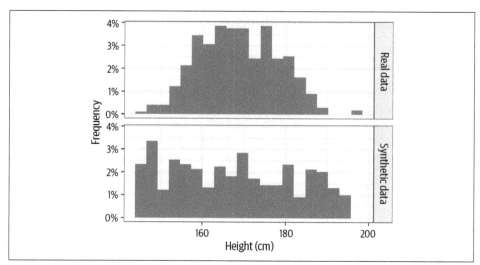

Figure 4-5. A comparison of real height data from a clinical trial and the synthesized version when the data synthesis did not work well

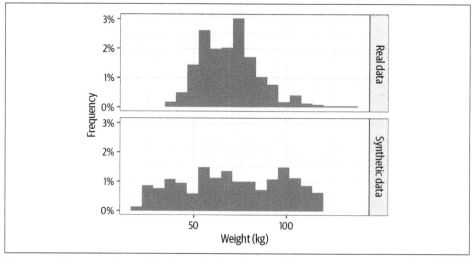

Figure 4-6. A comparison of real weight data from a clinical trial and the synthesized version when the data synthesis did not work well

In practice, there will be many variables in a dataset, and we want to be able to compare the real and synthetic distributions for all of them in a concise way. It is not practical to generate two histograms for every variable and visually compare them to decide if they are close enough or not: that is just not scalable and the reliability will not always be high (two analysts may assess the similarity of two distributions inconsistently). Therefore, we need some sort of summary statistic.

The Hellinger distance can be calculated to measure the difference in distribution between each variable in the real and synthetic data. The Hellinger distance is a probabilistic measure between 0 and 1, where 0 indicates no difference between distributions. It has been shown to behave in a manner consistent with other distribution comparison metrics when comparing original and transformed data (to protect data privacy).[6]

One important advantage of the Hellinger distance is that it is bounded, and that makes it easier to interpret. If the difference is close to 0, then we know that the distributions are similar, and if it is close to 1, then we know that they are very different. It can also be used to compare the univariate data utility for different data synthesis approaches. And another advantage is that it can be computed for continuous and categorical variables.

When we have many variables we can represent the Hellinger distances in a box-and-whisker plot, which shows the median and the inter-quartile range (IQR). This gives a good summary view of how similar the univariate distributions are between the real and synthetic data. The box-and-whisker plot shows the box bounded by the 75th and 25th percentiles, and the median is a line in the middle.

For a high-utility synthetic dataset, we expect the median Hellinger distance across all variables to be close to 0 and the variation to be small, indicating that the synthetic data replicates the distribution of each variable in the real data accurately.

Figure 4-7 summarizes the differences between the univariate distributions of the synthetic data relative to the real data for the first trial. The median Hellinger distance was 0.01 (IQR = 0.02), indicating that the distributions of real and synthetic variables were nearly identical. Figure 4-8 summarizes the differences in the univariate distribution of the synthetic data relative to the real data for the second trial. The median Hellinger distance was 0.02 (IQR = 0.03), also indicating that the real and synthetic variables were nearly identical in distribution.

---

6 Shanti Gomatam, Alan F. Karr, and Ashish P. Sanil, "Data Swapping as a Decision Problem," *Journal of Official Statistics* 21, no. 4 (2005): 635–55.

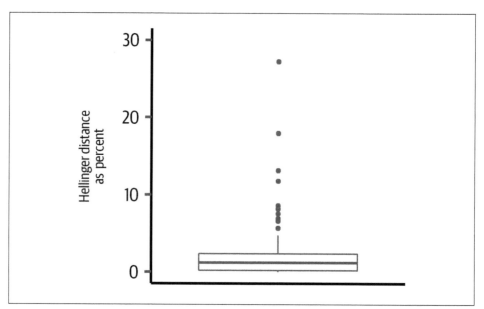

Figure 4-7. The Hellinger distance as percent for all variables in the dataset. This indicates how similar the univariate distributions are between the real and the synthetic data for the first trial.

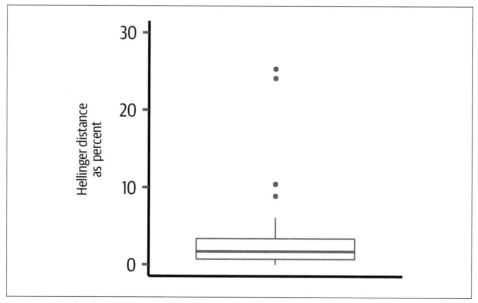

Figure 4-8. The Hellinger distance as percent for all variables in the dataset. This indicates how similar the univariate distributions are between the real and the synthetic data for the second trial.

Comparing Bivariate Statistics

Computing differences between correlations in the real and synthetic data is a commonly used approach for evaluating the utility of synthetic data.[7] In such a case, the absolute difference in correlations between all variable pairs in the real and synthetic data can be computed as a measure of data utility. We would want the correlations to be very similar between the two datasets.

The type of correlation coefficient will depend on the types of variables. For example, a different coefficient is needed for a correlation between two continuous variables versus a correlation between a binary variable and a categorical variable.

For relationships between continuous variables, Pearson correlation coefficients can be used. For correlation between continuous and nominal variables, the multiple correlation coefficient can be used, while for continuous and dichotomous variables, point-biserial correlation is used. If one of the variables is nominal and the other is nominal or dichotomous, Cramér's V can be used. Lastly, if both variables are dichotomous, the phi coefficient can be calculated to quantify correlation.

The absolute difference in bivariate correlations should then be scaled as necessary to ensure all difference values are bounded by 0 and 1. For a high-utility synthetic dataset, we would expect that the median absolute differences in these correlation measures calculated on the real data and on the synthetic data would be close to 0.

Again, to represent the utility in a concise manner, we can plot the absolute difference in correlations on a box-and-whisker plot across all possible pairwise relationships or we can represent these as a heat map. A heat map shows the difference value in shades to illustrate which bivariate correlation differences are big versus small.

---

7 Brett K. Beaulieu-Jones et al., "Privacy-Preserving Generative Deep Neural Networks Support Clinical Data Sharing," bioRxiv (July 2017). *https://doi.org/10.1101/159756*; Bill Howe et al., "Synthetic Data for Social Good," Cornell University arXiv Archive, October 2017. *https://arxiv.org/abs/1710.08874*; Ioannis Kaloskampis, "Synthetic Data for Public Good," Office for National Statistics, February 2019. *https://oreil.ly/qfVvR*.

Examining the difference in bivariate correlations for the first trial in Figure 4-9, the median absolute difference in the correlation observed in the real data compared to the correlation observed in the synthetic data was 0.03 (IQR = 0.04). In Figure 4-10, we have the results for the second trial, where the median absolute difference in the correlation observed in the synthetic data compared to the correlation observed in the real data was 0.03 (IQR = 0.04). This indicates that the bivariate relationships in the data have been broadly preserved during the synthetic data generation process.

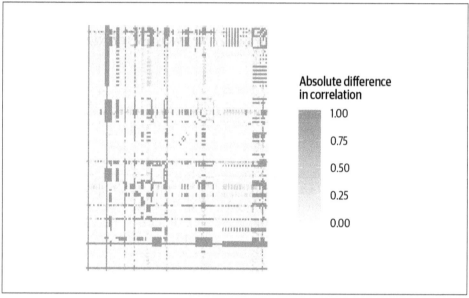

Figure 4-9. Absolute differences in bivariate correlations between the real and synthetic data for the first trial. Lighter shades indicate that the differences were close to 0, while gray corresponds to where correlation could not be computed due to missing values or low variability.

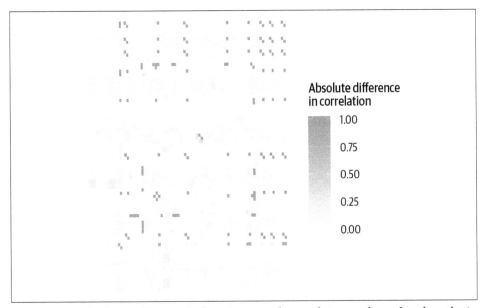

Figure 4-10. Absolute differences in bivariate correlations between the real and synthetic data for the second trial. Lighter shades indicate that the differences were close to 0, while gray corresponds to where correlation could not be computed due to missing values or low variability.

The box-and-whisker graphs for these differences are shown in Figures 4-11 and 4-12. These are more informative than the heat maps, although keep in mind that the box-and-whisker plots are summarizing thousands of bivariate correlations for every one of these datasets. For example, for the second trial there are 6,916 correlations actually computed from 7,056 possible correlations.

The outliers in this plot are the circles above the top whisker. In these datasets they occur because rare observations in the data can affect the correlation coefficients, or because some variables have many missing values which makes the correlation coefficients unstable. In general, we aim for a small median and consider all of the utility metrics together.

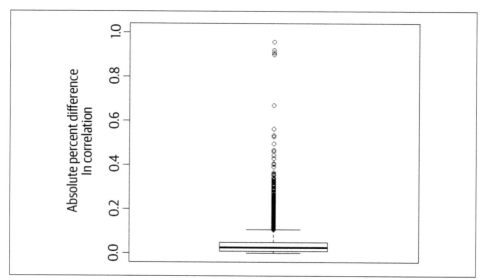

Figure 4-11. Absolute differences in bivariate correlations between the real and synthetic data for the first trial. The box-and-whisker plot illustrates the median and distributions clearly.

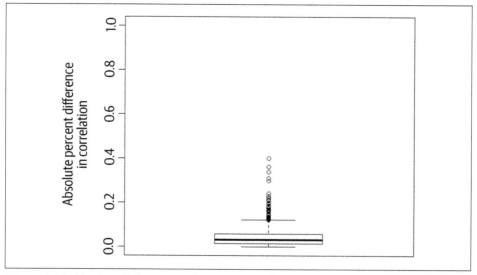

Figure 4-12. Absolute differences in bivariate correlations between the real and synthetic data for the second trial. The box-and-whisker plot illustrates the median and distributions clearly.

Comparing Multivariate Prediction Models

To determine whether the real and synthetic data have similar predictive ability using multivariate models, we can build classification models with every variable in the dataset as an outcome. Since it is not known a priori what an actual analyst would want to do with the dataset, we examine all possible models. This is called the *all models test*.

Generalized boosted models (GBM) can be used to build classification trees. These can produce quite accurate prediction models in practice.

A Description of ROCs

The receiver operating characteristics (ROC) curve is a way to measure how well a prediction model is performing. It addresses some of the problems with other common measures, especially with unbalanced datasets. This sidebar describes how ROCs work for binary predictions.

When predictions are made, they can be classified into a confusion matrix, as illustrated in Figure 4-13. The values are computed from running the prediction model on a test dataset that was not used in building the model. In this example the model is predicting a 0 or 1 value.

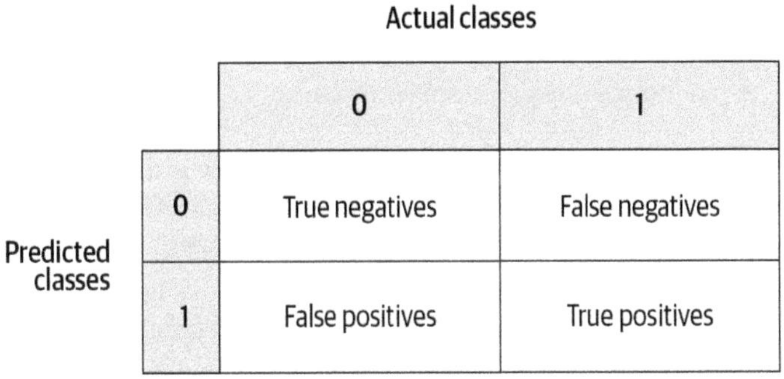

| | Actual classes | |
	0	1
Predicted classes — 0	True negatives	False negatives
Predicted classes — 1	False positives	True positives

Figure 4-13. A confusion matrix

For many binary prediction models, the actual prediction is a probability. For example, a classification tree or logistic regression will predict the probability that a particular observation is in the class labeled *1*. This probability is converted into a binary value by specifying a cutoff value, c. For example, if the cutoff is 0.5, then any predicted probability equal to or larger than 0.5 would be put into class *1*.

The ROC curve plots the values of the True Positive Fraction against the values of the False Positive Fraction for all possible values of c. An example of an ROC curve is shown in Figure 4-14. The diagonal line indicates a useless prediction that is equal to tossing a coin. Lines B and C are better than chance. The closer the line is to the top left corner, the more accurate the predictions.

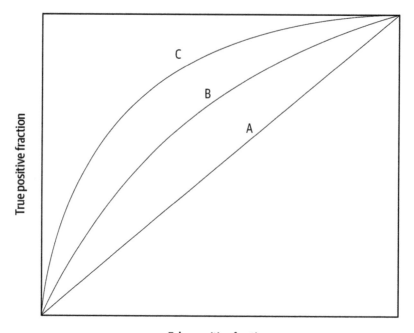

False positive fraction

Figure 4-14. A receiver operating characteristics curve

A common measure of overall performance of a classifier is the area under the ROC curve (or AUROC). This measure can be used to compare different classifiers or prediction models. In our case, we used the AUROC to compare the accuracy of models built using real versus synthetic data.

We needed to compute the accuracy of the models that we built. To do that, we used the area under the receiver operating characteristics curve (known as the AUROC; see "A Description of ROCs").[8] The AUROC is a standardized way to evaluate prediction model accuracy. To compute the AUROC we used 10-fold cross-validation. This is when we split the dataset into multiple training and testing subsets.

---

8 Margaret Sullivan Pepe, *The Statistical Evaluation of Medical Tests for Classification and Prediction* (Oxford: Oxford University Press, 2004).

Let's describe 10-fold cross-validation briefly. We take a dataset and split it into 10 equally sized subsets numbered (1) to (10). We first keep subset (1) as a test set and build a model with the remaining nine subsets. We then test the model on the subset (1) that we took out. We compute the AUROC on that test set. We then put subset (1) back in as part of the training data and take subset (2) out and use it for testing, and we compute AUROC for that. The process is repeated 10 times, each time taking one of the subsets out and using it for testing. At the end we have 10 values for AUROC. We take the average of these to compute the overall AUROC.

This average AUROC was computed for every model we built on the synthetic data and its counterpart on the real data (the counterpart being a model with the same outcome variable). The absolute difference between the two AUROC values was computed. A box-and-whisker plot was then generated from all of these absolute differences in the AUROC values.

To ensure that all of the models can be summarized in a consistent way, continuous outcome variables can be discretized to build the classification models. We used univariate k-means clustering, with optimal cluster sizes chosen by the majority rule.[9] High-utility synthetic data would have little difference in predictive ability compared to the real data, indicated by the median percent difference in mean AUROC.

Figure 4-15 shows the results of 10-fold cross-validation to assess the predictive accuracy of each GBM for the first trial. The absolute percent difference in the AUROC is near 0 for many variables, with a median of 0.5% (IQR = 3%). This indicates that analysis conducted using the synthetic data instead of the real dataset has very similar predictive ability, and that generally the models trained using synthetic data will produce the same conclusion when applied to real data as models that were trained using real data.

In Figure 4-16 we have a similar result for the second trial. The absolute percent difference in the AUROC has a median of 0.02% (IQR = 1%). This also indicates that the synthetic data has very similar predictive ability to the real data.

---

9 Malika Charrad et al., "NbClust: An R Package for Determining the Relevant Number of Clusters in a Data Set," *Journal of Statistical Software* 61, no. 6 (November 2014): 1–36.

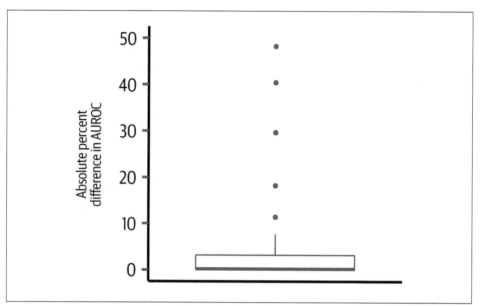

Figure 4-15. Absolute percent difference between the real and synthetic models for the first trial

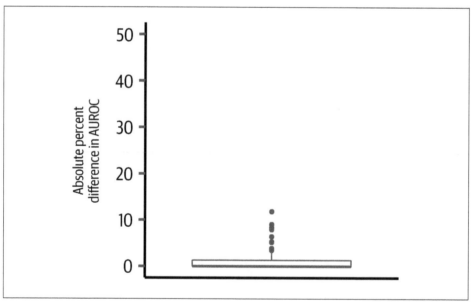

Figure 4-16. Absolute percent difference between the real and synthetic models for the second trial

Another approach, which we will refer to as an external validation of sorts, is as follows:

1. Divide the real data into 10 equally sized random segments.
2. Remove segment one and make it a test set, and generate the synthetic data on the remaining nine segments.
3. Build a GBM using the synthetic data and predict on the test segment from the real data and compute the AUROC.
4. Repeat the process another nine times with each segment taken out as the test set.
5. Once all predictions have been made across the 10 folds, compute the average AUROC.

This multivariate external validation tests whether the synthesized data can generate good predictive models where the goodness is evaluated on the holdout real data.

Distinguishability

Distinguishability is another way to compare real and synthetic data in a multivariate manner. We want to see if we can build a model that can distinguish between real and synthetic records. Therefore, we assign a binary indicator to each record, with a 1 if it is a real record and a 0 if it is a synthetic record (or vice versa). We then build a classification model that discriminates between real and synthetic data. We use this model to predict whether a record is real or synthetic. We can use a 10-fold cross-validation approach to come up with a prediction for each record.

This classifier can output a probability for each prediction. If the probability is closer to 1, then it is predicting that a record is real. If the probability is closer to 0, then it is predicting that a record is synthetic. This is effectively a *propensity score* for every record.

In health research settings, the propensity score is typically used to balance treatment groups in observational studies when random assignment to the treatment (versus the control) is not possible. It provides a single probabilistic measure that weighs the effect of multiple covariates on the receipt of treatment in these observational studies.[10] Using the propensity score as a measure to distinguish between real and

---

10 Paul R. Rosenbaum and Donald B. Rubin, "The Central Role of the Propensity Score in Observational Studies for Causal Effects," *Biometrika* 70, no. 1 (April 1983): 41–55.

synthetic data is becoming a somewhat common practice.[11] Propensity scores can be computed quite accurately using generalized boosted models.[12]

If the two datasets are exactly the same, then there will be no distinguishability between them—this is when the synthetic data generator was overfit and effectively re-created the original data. In such a case the propensity score of every record will be 0.5, in that the classifier is not able to distinguish between real and synthetic data. This is illustrated in Figure 4-17. In the same manner, if the label of "real" versus "synthetic" is assigned to the records completely at random, then the classifier will not be able to distinguish between them. In such a case the propensity score will also be 0.5.

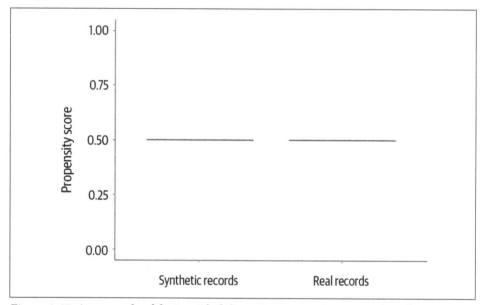

Figure 4-17. An example of distinguishability using propensity scores when there is no difference between real and synthetic data

If the two datasets are completely different, then the classifier will be able to distinguish between them. High distinguishability means that the data utility is low. In such a case the propensity score will be either 0 or 1, as illustrated in Figure 4-18.

11 Joshua Snoke et al., "General and Specific Utility Measures for Synthetic Data," *Journal of the Royal Statistical Society: Series A (Statistics in Society)* 181, no. 3 (June 2018): 663–688.

12 Daniel F. McCaffrey et al., "A Tutorial on Propensity Score Estimation for Multiple Treatments Using Generalized Boosted Models," *Statistics in Medicine* 32, no. 19 (2013): 3388–3414.

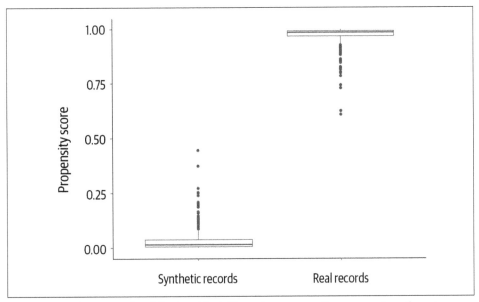

Figure 4-18. An example of distinguishability using propensity scores when there is almost a perfect difference between real and synthetic data

Of course, in reality, datasets will fall somewhere in between. We would not want them to be at either of these two extremes. Synthetic data that is difficult to distinguish from real data is considered to have relatively high utility.

We can also summarize this propensity score across all records. There are a few general methods that can be used for doing so (we call them the propensity score for synthesis, or PSS, 1 to 3):

PSS1: computing the mean square difference between the propensity score and the 0.5 value

The 0.5 value is what the value would be if there were no difference between the real and synthetic data. It is also the expected value if labels were assigned randomly. Therefore, such a propensity mean square difference would have a value of 0 if the two datasets were the same, and a value of 0.25 if they were different.

PSS2: converting the propensity score into a binary prediction

If the propensity score is greater than 0.5, predict that it is a real record. If the propensity score is less than 0.5, predict that it is a synthetic record. If the propensity score is 0.5, toss a coin. After that, compute the accuracy of these predictions. The accuracy will be closer to 1 if the two datasets are very different, which means that the classifier is able to distinguish perfectly between the real and synthetic data. The accuracy will be closer to 0.5 if the classifier is not able to distinguish between the two datasets.[13]

PSS3: computing the mean square difference between the propensity score and the actual 0/1 label of a record

In such a case the difference will be 0 if the classifier is able to distinguish perfectly between the two datasets, and 0.25 if it is unable to distinguish between the datasets.

A summary of these different metrics is provided in Table 4-1.

Table 4-1. The different summary statistics for the propensity score

Type of metric	Datasets the same	Datasets different
Mean square difference from 0.5	0	0.25
Accuracy of prediction	0.5	1
Mean square difference from label	0.25	0

In general we prefer to use the mean square difference from 0.5 or PSS1, but in practice all three methods will provide similar conclusions about data utility.

The comparison on the propensity score for the first trial indicates that generalized boosted models are not able to confidently distinguish the real data from the synthetic (see Figure 4-19). For the second trial, see Figure 4-20. In both cases the PSS1 scores are close to 0.1.

---

13 This metric is not suitable if the data is not balanced. For example, this will happen when the synthesized dataset is much larger than the real dataset.

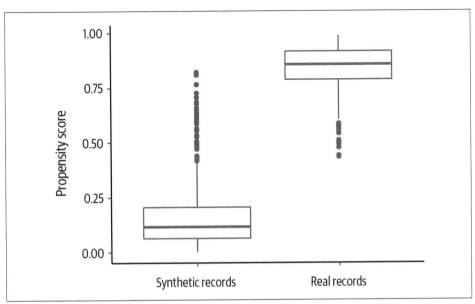

Figure 4-19. The propensity scores computed for the first trial, contrasting the values for real versus synthetic data

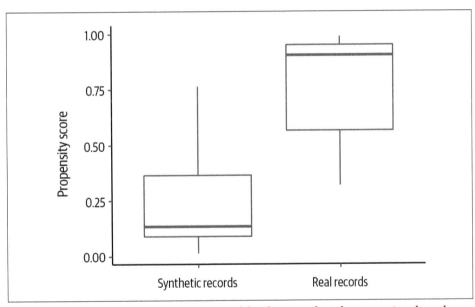

Figure 4-20. The propensity scores computed for the second trial, contrasting the values for real versus synthetic data

This result is a bit different than what we saw for the same datasets under the "all models" utility evaluation. That is not surprising because the utility tests are measuring different things. One possible explanation is as follows. The multivariate "all models" test selects the most important variables to build the model. It is plausible that variable importance varies between the real and synthetic datasets in these models but that the overall prediction is equivalent. In the PSS1 measure, the possibility that some variables are less/more important for some prediction tasks will be captured.

This highlights the importance of considering multiple utility metrics in order to get a broader appreciation of the utility of the dataset. Each method for assessing utility is covering a different dimension of utility that is complementary to the others.

We need a way to interpret these values. For example, is a PSS1 value of 0.1 good or bad?

One way to interpret the PSS1 score is to split the range into quintiles, as shown in Figure 4-21. We would ideally want the score to be at level 1, or at most at level 2, to ensure that the utility of the dataset is adequate. This also provides an easy-to-interpret approach to compare the distinguishability of different synthesis methods and datasets.

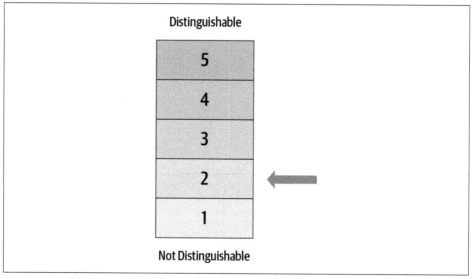

Figure 4-21. *The PSS1 range can be split into quintiles, with a value closer to level 1 showing less distinguishability*

Summary

The growing application and acceptance of synthetic data is evidenced by the plan to generate the heavily used general-purpose public tabulations from the US 2020 decennial census from synthetic data.[14] A key question from synthetic data users is about its data utility. This chapter presented and demonstrated a framework to assess the utility of synthetic data, combining both generic and workload-aware measures.

A replicated analysis of a US census dataset showed that an original analysis could be replicated with high precision. This is an example of evaluating the utility when the eventual workload is known reasonably well in advance.

The utility analysis on two oncology trial datasets showed that by a variety of metrics, the synthetic datasets replicate the structure and distributions, as well as the bivariate and multivariate relationships of the real datasets reasonably well. While it uses only two studies, it does provide some initial evidence that it is possible to generate analytically useful synthetic clinical trial data. Such a framework can provide value for data users, data synthesizers, and researchers working on data synthesis methods.

The results of a utility assessment can be summarized in a dashboard, as in Figure 4-22. This gives in a single picture the key metrics on utility.

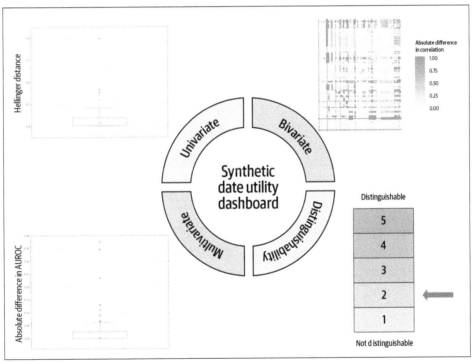

Figure 4-22. A dashboard summarizing the utility metrics for a synthetic dataset

14 Aref Dajani et al., "The Modernization of Statistical Disclosure Limitation at the U.S. Census Bureau" (presentation at the Census Scientific Advisory Committee meeting, Suitland, MD, September 2017).

In terms of limitations of the framework, we examined all variables and all models in our utility framework, then summarized across these. In practice, some of these variables or models may be more important than others, and will be driven by the question being addressed in the analysis. However, this framework still provides more meaningful results than generic data utility metrics, which would not reflect all workloads.

Note that in this chapter we focused on cross-sectional data. For longitudinal data, other types of utility metrics may be needed. This is a more complex topic because it is more dependent on the type of data (e.g., health data versus financial data).

In the next chapter, we examine in more detail how to generate synthetic data. Now that we know how to assess data utility, we can more easily compare alternative synthesis methods.

CHAPTER 5

Methods for Synthesizing Data

After describing some basic methods for distribution fitting in the last chapter, we will now use these concepts to generate synthetic data. We will start off with some basic approaches and build up to some more complex ones as the chapter progresses. We will refer to more advanced techniques later on that are beyond the scope of an introductory text, but what we cover should give you a good introduction.

Generating Synthetic Data from Theory

Let's consider the situation where the analyst does not have any real data to start off with, but has some understanding of the phenomenon that they want to model and generate data for. For example, let's say that we want to generate data reflecting the relationship between height and weight. It is generally known that height and weight are positively associated.

According to the Centers for Disease Control, the average height for men in the US is approximately 175 cm,[1] and for the sake of our example we will assume a standard deviation of 5 cm. The average weight is 89.7 kg, and we will assume a standard deviation of 10 kg. For the sake of our example, we will model these as normal (Gaussian or bell-shaped) distributions and assume that the correlation between them is 0.5. According to Cohen's guidelines for the interpretation of effect sizes, a correlation of magnitude equal to 0.5 is considered to be large, 0.3 is considered to be medium, and 0.1 is considered to be small. Any correlation above 0.5 would be a strong correlation

---

1 Cheryl D. Fryar et al., "Mean Body Weight, Height, Waist Circumference, and Body Mass Index Among Adults: United States, 1999–2000 Through 2015–2016," National Center for Health Statistics, December 2018. *https://oreil.ly/bgf9i.*

in practice.[2] Therefore, at 0.5 we are assuming a large correlation between height and weight. Based on these specifications, we can create a dataset of 5,000 observations that models this phenomenon.

We will present three ways to do this: (a) sampling from multivariate (normal) distributions, (b) inducing a correlation during the sampling process, and (c) using copulas. Each will be illustrated below.

Sampling from a Multivariate Normal Distribution

In the first method, we generate data from these two distributions by sampling from the density function, and during the generation process we can ensure that the generated values of height and weight are correlated at 0.5. In this example we want to generate 5,000 synthetic observations. Because the two variables are normally distributed, we can sample from a multivariate normal distribution. When we do that, we end up with a two-variable dataset with 5,000 observations with a correlation of 0.5, which is shown in Figure 5-1.

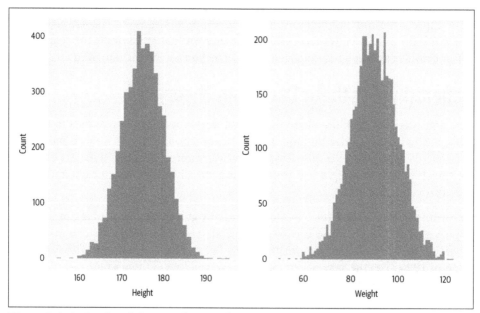

Figure 5-1. A simulated dataset of 5,000 observations consisting of height and weight generated from a multivariate normal distribution

---

2 Jacob Cohen, *Statistical Power Analysis for the Behavioral Sciences*, 2nd edition (Mahwah: Lawrence Erlbaum Associates, 1988).

That was easy. And the basic process can be extended to as many variables as we want (i.e., we are not limited to two variables).

Inducing Correlations with Specified Marginal Distributions

Now let's say that we want to generate data showing the relationship between a patient's weight and their length of stay (LOS) at the hospital. The length-of-stay variable has an exponential distribution, as illustrated in Figure 5-2. We will assume that the correlation is weak between these two variables—say, 0.1.

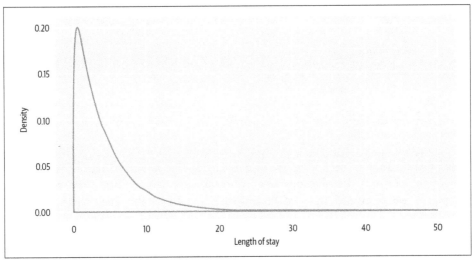

Figure 5-2. An exponential distribution representing the length of stay

Sampling from a multivariate normal distribution works well when we know that the distributions of the variables are normal. But what if they are not, as in the current example? We cannot generate this synthetic data from a multivariate normal because the length-of-stay variable is not a normal distribution.

In that case, we can sample from the normal and exponential distributions but at the same time induce the desired correlation during the sampling process.[3] We then have the synthetic data distributions in Figure 5-3 with an actual correlation between them that was computed at 0.094, which is quite close to the desired correlation of 0.1.

This basic process can be further expanded to multiple variables. We can specify a correlation matrix of bivariate relationships among multiple variables and use the same process to induce the desired correlations as we are sampling.

---

3 Ronald L. Iman and W. J. Conover, "A Distribution-Free Approach to Inducing Rank Correlation Among Input Variables," *Communications in Statistics - Simulation and Computation* 11, no. 3 (1982): 311–334.

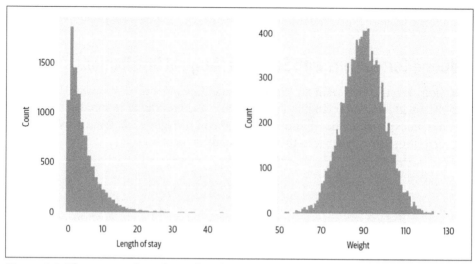

Figure 5-3. The generated synthetic data for weight and length of stay by inducing a correlation when sampling

This process can work well if we are able to specify the data distributions in terms of one of the classical distributions (e.g., normal, exponential, Beta, and so on). In Chapter 3 we discussed ways of finding the best fit of real data to the classical distributions.

Copulas with Known Marginal Distributions

Another approach for generating synthetic data is to use copulas to model marginal distributions that are different and still maintain the correlations among them. A key characteristic of copulas is that they separate the definition of the marginal distributions from the correlation structure, and they still allow the sampling from these distributions to create new data while maintaining the correlation structure.

In our last example we had two marginal distributions, a normal distribution and an exponential distribution. For our purposes, we will use a Gaussian copula. With a Gaussian copula we would generate observations from a standard multivariate normal distribution with a correlation of 0.1, and then map the generated values to our normal and exponential distributions through the cumulative density functions (CDF). This is called a *probability integral transform*. We compute the CDFs from standard multivariate normal distribution, and then compute the quantiles back to our exponential and normal distributions for LOS and weight. By using copulas we sampled 5,000 observations for the two distributions, and these are shown in Figure 5-4 with an actual 0.094 correlation between them, which is very close to the desired correlation.

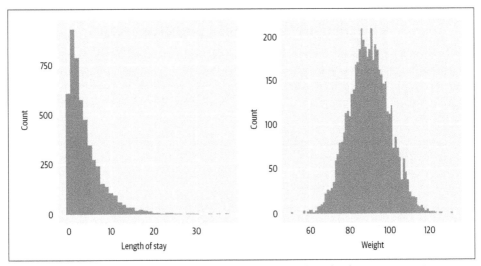

Figure 5-4. The generated synthetic data for weight and length of stay using a Gaussian copula

Again, the concept behind copulas can be extended to multiple variables, and when their marginal distributions are specified, the generated datasets will generally maintain the marginal distributions and bivariate correlations, even when the distributions are quite different from each other.

We are not limited to 5,000 observations. When generating the datasets, we can do so for much larger datasets, or very small datasets. The generated sample size will be a function of the analyst's needs.

In the next section we will look at the case when we have real data and we want to synthesize data from that. In such a case, we do not have theoretical distributions to work from. This can happen when the phenomenon is complex or not well understood.

Generating Realistic Synthetic Data

When there is real data available, then the process described previously can be applied. The main difference is that we need to generate synthetic data based on a model of real datasets and not theoretical relationships. We will use an example of a hospital discharge dataset to illustrate this process. This example dataset is detailed in "A Description of the Hospital Discharge Dataset."

A Description of the Hospital Discharge Dataset

Whenever a patient is discharged, all the data related to that patient's experience at the hospital is aggregated and put into standardized discharge databases. These databases are very important for analyzing healthcare system performance and costs, quality improvement, and public health, among other reasons. This data is called discharge abstracts or summaries.

The dataset we use is for one year and comes from one US state. We consider only three variables:

- Age at the time of discharge (AGE)
- Number of days since last service (DSLS), which indicates how many days ago a patient last received service at the hospital
- Length of stay (LOS), which indicates how many days a patient was in the hospital

An AGE of 0 means that this was a birth. A DSLS of 0 means that this was a first admission. A LOS of 0 means that the patient did not stay overnight at the hospital. The distributions of these three variables is shown in Figure 5-5. There are a total of 189,042 observations in this dataset.

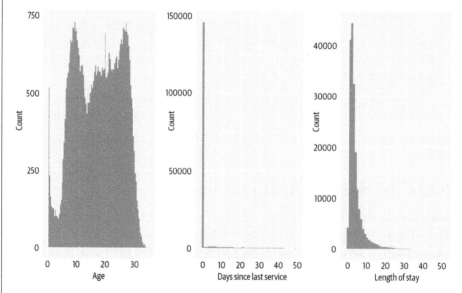

Figure 5-5. Density of the three variables in the hospital discharge dataset that we are using for illustrative purposes. Note that the y-axes are not the same for the three graphs.

We will need to fit the marginal distributions in our data to some kind of classical distribution. We discussed distribution fitting in more detail in Chapter 3. Therefore, we are still generating data from classical distributions, except that these distributions are derived from best fits with real data.

Fitting Real Data to Known Distributions

For our three hospital variables, we will first fit them to classic distributions. We determined that AGE follows a Beta distribution (multiplied by a constant, which in this case was approximately 100) and that both DSLS and LOS follow an exponential distribution. Then to generate the synthetic data we can sample from the fitted distributions, as described previously, and induce the same correlations as the original data.[4] The sampling process can generate synthetic datasets of any size (the synthetic data can be much larger or smaller than the original data).

This process gives us the correlations in Figure 5-6. As you can see, the synthetic data correlations are quite close to the real correlations.

	AGE	DSLS	LOS
AGE	1	0.1617 (0.165)	0.1968 (0.223)
DSLS	0.1617 (0.165)	1	0.1424 (0.168)
LOS	0.1968 (0.223)	0.1424 (0.168)	1

Figure 5-6. A correlation matrix giving a comparison between the original correlations and the synthetic correlations for pairs of variables in the hospital discharge data. The values in parentheses are the original correlations, and the values above them are the induced correlations in the synthesized data.

The problem here is that the fitted distributions (Beta and exponential) are not good fits to the real data. We can see that in Table 5-1. These were the best distributions from the most common known ones that we could fit with. In that table, the Hellinger distance is an interpretable measure of how similar the distributions are.

---

4 Ronald L. Iman and W. J. Conover, "A Distribution-Free Approach to Inducing Rank Correlation Among Input Variables," *Communications in Statistics - Simulation and Computation* 11, no. 3 (1982): 311–334.

Table 5-1. The Hellinger distances between the samples from the fitted distributions and the real variables from the hospital discharge dataset

Variable	Hellinger distance
AGE	0.972
DSLS	0.910
LOS	0.917

Let's try doing the same thing with Gaussian copulas, where we generate synthetic data that matches the fitted distributions from the real data. The correlations among the variables are shown in Figure 5-7. As can be seen, the generated data does maintain the correlations quite well.

	AGE	DSLS	LOS
AGE	1	0.157 (0.165)	0.208 (0.223)
DSLS	0.157 (0.165)	1	0.164 (0.168)
LOS	0.208 (0.223)	0.164 (0.168)	1

Figure 5-7. A comparison between the original correlations and the synthetic correlations for pairs of variables in the hospital discharge data. The values in parentheses are the original correlations, and the values above them are the correlations using data generated with a Gaussian copula.

The Hellinger distances for the marginal distributions generated using the Gaussian copula are the same as shown in Table 5-1. The conclusion is the same as before: the fits are not that convincing.

Therefore, when we try to fit classic distributions to real data, the fits may be the best available, but that does not mean that they will be very good. Of course, the veracity of that last statement will be data dependent, but we work with complex health and consumer data, and we often see poor fits. We need to find a repeatable and scalable solution that will work for all kinds of real data.

Using Machine Learning to Fit the Distributions

As we saw in the previous chapter, we can use machine learning models to fit the distributions. This allows us to build a model that can generate synthetic data that more

---

faithfully reflects the real distributions in the data. With these ML fitted distributions, we can then apply these distributions with the methods of inducing a correlation and with copulas.

The similarity between the fitted distributions and the real distributions is quite high, as illustrated in Table 5-2. We can use these fitted models to generate marginal distributions of any size.

Table 5-2. The Hellinger distances for the synthetic marginal distributions using a machine learning method for fitting a model to the real marginal distributions

Variable	Hellinger distance
AGE	0.0001
DSLS	0.001
LOS	0.04

We will now also use the distinguishability metric that we discussed in the utility chapter. This tells us how similar the synthetic dataset is to the real dataset. The summary in Table 5-3 shows the distinguishability metric for the three approaches. With the methods of inducing correlations during sampling and Gaussian copulas, we used the ML fitted distributions instead of the known distributions. As can be seen, the distinguishability is low across the board, and all of the methods produce very comparable results.

Table 5-3. The distinguishability between the real and synthetic data when distributions fitted to the real data using machine learning models are used

Method	Distinguishability
Inducing correlations	0.005
Gaussian copulas	0.02
Decision trees	0.003

The key lesson here is that the machine learning models are far superior to modeling distributions of real datasets. They will generally outperform trying to fit real data to classic distributions.

Hybrid Synthetic Data

Now let's consider the situation where we want to create *hybrid data*. This is where one part of the synthetic data is based on real data, and the second part is based on a theoretical understanding of the phenomenon, but we do not actually have data. In essence, this is adding signal to the data.

Taking our example of the hospital data, let's add a new variable indicating the number of cigarettes smoked and then synthesize the dataset using a Gaussian copula. This would have an exponential distribution where 86% of individuals do not smoke (ensuring consistency with the general population). The assumed correlations that we have added to the original data are shown in Figure 5-8. Here we assumed that there is a weak positive correlation with age, and a moderate negative correlation with DSLS, and a moderate positive correlation with LOS. The real data correlations are shown in parentheses in the diagram. As can be seen, the overall correlation structure has been maintained quite well in the data that was synthesized.

	AGE	DSLS	LOS	Smoking
AGE	1	(0.164) 0.12	(0.222) 0.21	(0.1) 0.093
DSLS	(0.164) 0.12	1	(0.162) 0.12	(-0.3) -0.22
LOS	(0.222) 0.209	(0.162) 0.12	1	(0.3) 0.28
Smoking	(0.1) 0.093	(-0.3) -0.22	(0.3) 0.28	1

Figure 5-8. The correlation matrix showing real and synthetic data that was generated using a copula. The values in parentheses are the original correlations, and the values below them are the induced correlations in the synthesized data.

We can now use the methods that were examined earlier to synthesize a dataset that is partially based on real data and has additional signals added to it, while maintaining the original correlations. Again, we can see the Hellinger distances comparing the synthetic distributions to the real data for the three real variables using both methods in Table 5-4.

Table 5-4. The Hellinger distances for the synthetic marginal distributions using a Gaussian copula to generate the hybrid data

Variable	Hellinger distance
AGE	0.0036
DSLS	0.004
LOS	0.007
Smoking	0.006

This synthetic dataset merged real information with hypothetical information to generate a hybrid. The basic principles can be easily extended to more variables and used with other techniques.

The set of methods we have described here provides a toolbox for the generation of artificial, realistic, and hybrid data. Furthermore, the methods can be extended to an arbitrary number of variables to create quite complex datasets.

Sequential Machine Learning Synthesis

One way to generate synthetic data is to build on commonly used regression and classification algorithms. Commonly used algorithms are classification and regression trees (CARTs),[5] although variants of these can also be used. Other algorithms, such as support vector machines, can be used as well. For the sake of illustration, we will assume that CART is being used for synthesis.

Let's say we have five variables, A, B, C, D, and E. The generation is performed sequentially, and therefore we need to have a sequence. Various criteria can be used to choose a sequence. For our example, we define the sequence as $A \rightarrow E \rightarrow C \rightarrow B \rightarrow D$.

Let the prime notation indicate that the variable is synthesized. For example, A' means that this is the synthesized version of A. The following are the steps for sequential generation:

- Sample from the A distribution to get A'
- Build a model F1: $E \sim A$
- Synthesize E as $E' = F1(A')$
- Build a model F2: $C \sim A + E$
- Synthesize C as $C' = F2(A', E')$
- Build a model F3: $B \sim A + E + C$
- Synthesize B as $B' = F3(A', E', C')$
- Build a model F4: $D \sim A + E + C + B$
- Synthesize D as $D' = F4(A', E', C', B')$

The process can be thought of as initially fitting a series of models {F1, F2, F3, F4}. These models make up the generator. Then these models can be used to generate data. When a model is used to generate data, we sample from the predicted terminal node to get the synthetic values. The distribution in the node can be smoothed before sampling.

---

5 Leo Breiman et al., *Classification and Regression Trees* (Milton Park: Taylor & Francis, 1984).

Machine Learning Methods

We will examine a representative machine learning method for the generation of synthetic data. We will use a decision tree, although any kind of regression and classification method can be used. The principle for each is the same in that we sequentially synthesize variables using classification and regression models. For the decision tree we use CART (see "Sequential Machine Learning Synthesis" on page 105).

The marginal distribution results on our hospital discharge data are shown in Table 5-5. Here we can see quite a good match between the synthesized distributions and the original ones.

Table 5-5. The Hellinger distances for the synthetic marginal distributions using a machine learning method to generate all of the synthetic datasets

Variable	Hellinger distance
AGE	0.0033
DSLS	0.005
LOS	0.0042

We can similarly see concordant correlations between the synthetic and the original data. Therefore, the tree was able to retain a good amount of the data utility. The distinguishability metric was 0.003, which is also quite low, indicating that the synthetic data retained much of the structure of the original data. See the matrix in Figure 5-9, which illustrates the correlation between variables in the original and synthetic datasets.

	AGE	DSLS	LOS
AGE	1	0.164 (0.165)	0.222 (0.223)
DSLS	0.164 (0.165)	1	0.162 (0.168)
LOS	0.222 (0.223)	0.162 (0.168)	1

Figure 5-9. The correlation matrix for the hospital data generated using a decision tree. The values in parentheses are the original correlations, and the values above them are the induced correlations in the synthesized data.

Deep Learning Methods

There are two general types of artificial neural network architectures that have been used to generate synthetic data. Both can work well, and in some cases they have been combined.

The first is the variational autoencoder (VAE). It is an unsupervised method to learn a meaningful representation of a multidimensional dataset. It first compresses the dataset into a more compact representation with fewer dimensions, which is often a multivariate Gaussian distribution. This acts as a bottleneck. The encoder performs that initial transformation. Then the decoder takes that compressed representation and reconstructs the original input data, as illustrated in Figure 5-10. The VAE is trained by optimizing the similarity between the decoded data and the input data. In this context, a VAE functions similarly to principal component analysis, except that it is able to capture nonlinear relationships in the data.

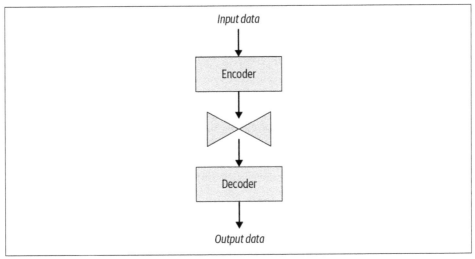

Figure 5-10. A high-level view of how a VAE works

Another architecture is the generative adversarial network (GAN). With a GAN there are two components, a generator and a discriminator. The generator network takes as input random data, often sampled from a normal or uniform distribution, and synthetic data is generated. The discriminator compares the synthetic data with the real data—creating a propensity score similar to what we saw before. The output of that discrimination is then fed back to train the generator. A good synthetic model is created when the discriminator is unable to distinguish between the real and synthetic datasets. A GAN architecture is shown in Figure 5-11.

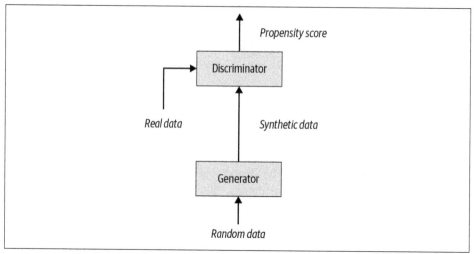

Figure 5-11. A high-level view of how a GAN works

Both of these approaches have demonstrated quite high synthesis utility on complex datasets and are a very active area of research.

Synthesizing Sequences

Many datasets consist of sequences of events that need to be modeled. Here we will assume that the dataset has a series of discrete events. For example, the dataset may consist of healthcare encounters, such as visiting a doctor, getting a lab test done, going to get a prescription, and so on. An example of such a dataset is illustrated in the data model in Figure 5-12.

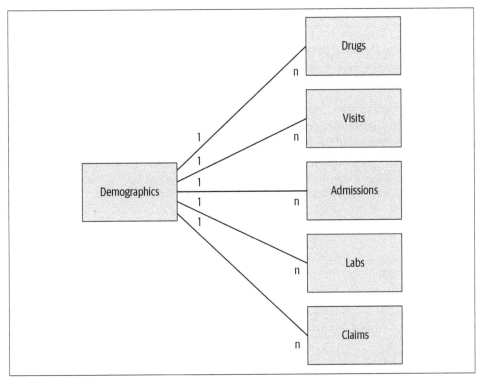

Figure 5-12. An example of a complex health dataset with multiple sequences

Here we have a relational data model with some patient demographics for each patient. Then there are possibly multiple events reflecting the drugs that have been prescribed to that patient over time. There can also be multiple events per patient, one for each visit to the clinic. A patient may be admitted more than once to the hospital over the period of the data collection. There may also be multiple lab tests and insurance claims per patient. Thus in the dataset there will be multiple events occurring per individual over time.

Some of these events, such as death, may end the sequence; or, if the event is a study, there can be another event signifying the end of the study. In many cases, these datasets will also be ordered.

To synthesize this dataset, we need to first compute the transition matrix among all of the events. This can be estimated empirically by looking at the proportion of times that a particular event follows another one. For instance, let's say that we have four events A, B, C, and D. And let's say that C is a terminal event, in that nothing comes after C in terms of outgoing transitions. If 40% of the time an event B follows an event A, then we can say that the transition from A to B has a probability of 0.4.

Creating such a transition matrix assumes that an event is dependent on only one previous event. This can be quite limiting, and the synthesis will not be able to capture longer-term trends. Therefore, we can assume that an event depends on the previous two events (or more—that is a design decision; for our purposes though we will assume that we want to capture two previous events).

An example of a transition matrix is shown in Figure 5-13. Here we have the two previous events, in a particular order because in a healthcare context the order will matter, along with the transition probabilities. The rows indicate the previous states, and the columns indicate the next state. Each row needs to add up to 1 because the sum of the total transitions from a pair of consecutive states must be 1. Also, there are no previous states with a C event in them because that is a terminal event.

	A	B	C	D
AB	0.31	0.29	0.39	0.00
BA	0.42	0.21	0.22	0.16
AD	0.64	0.11	0.08	0.18
DA	0.38	0.05	0.23	0.34
BD	0.41	0.31	0.26	0.02
DB	0.01	0.16	0.57	0.26

Figure 5-13. An example of a transition matrix with four events, with C being a terminal event and an order of two

For every individual that we want to synthesize for, we need to determine the start state. The start state can be synthesized from other data. But this is still not sufficient. We need to construct another transition matrix from the start state to the second state. This is illustrated in Figure 5-14. This acts as a "starter" transition matrix.

	A	B	C	D
A	0.20	0.40	0.30	0.10
B	0.36	0.34	0.25	0.04
D	0.34	0.48	0.17	0.01

Figure 5-14. An example of a transition matrix for starting the generation sequence

For each patient, we can begin from their starting state and then select the next state randomly according to the transition probabilities. For example, if the starter state is A, then there is a 40% chance that the next state is B. Let's say that B was selected. Then we have a sequence of AB. We then start from the AB row (Figure 5-13) in the second transition matrix and go on a random walk through that matrix until we hit a terminal node. For example, after AB we may randomly select another A event. Now the previous two events are BA, which may lead to a C event, and that would be the end of the sequence for that individual. This is repeated for however many sequences we want to generate.

Once a sequence is generated, we can compute the Hellinger distance between each row of the synthetic transition matrix and the real data matrix to evaluate how similar that sequence is to the original data. A median across all rows would provide an overall measure of similarity of sequences.

This approach works well but has some limitations, which we will summarize in the following paragraphs.

The example we looked at considered only two historical events. For complex datasets, the history that needs to be taken into account would be larger, otherwise the generated utility may be limited. We can create transition matrices with more history, of course. This can be done if there is sufficient data to estimate or compute the transition probabilities; otherwise, these can be somewhat unstable.

Another common challenge is that some events do not have an order that is discernible from the data. For example, during a hospital visit, there may be lab tests and diagnostic imaging events. The data will likely capture these events not by the minute but by the day. Therefore, all of these events effectively occurred at the same time.

The interval between events would need to be considered as well. For example, some events will happen a week apart, and some will happen months apart. The interval may not be fixed (of course, that will depend on the dataset). In a health dataset, for example, these intervals can vary quite a bit between events for the same individual.

And the interval information is very important because many analyses will look at time to event (for example, the survival time of cancer patients).

Finally, the events may have additional attributes associated with them. For example, a lab test event will have the results of the lab test associated with that event. We did not consider these attributes in this description.

Therefore, modeling sequence, or longitudinal, data in the manner described previously is a good starting point, but it has limitations hat would require more advanced techniques to be applied. For this type of data, recurrent neural networks would be a good way to model the sequences and take into account more of the history.

Summary

In this chapter, we outlined a few methods that are relatively straightforward to implement for data synthesis and that in practice will give good results in terms of data utility. We also provided some direction for handling sequential data.

As a general recommendation, data synthesis with machine learning methods will provide better data utility than inducing correlated data and using copulas, although the latter are both useful techniques to have available for simpler datasets.

When datasets get more complex, machine learning and deep learning methods will perform better. Furthermore, there are no real practical techniques to handle high data complexity except machine learning and deep learning models. There has not, however, been a comprehensive comparison of these methods. Different analysts choose a method they prefer and continuously optimize it.

Important criteria for choosing a synthesis method are that it works with the types of data that you need to synthesize and that it does not require extensive tuning to work.

There are small datasets, for example, with which deep learning techniques may struggle to perform well. In such cases, statistical machine learning techniques could be a good option. Also, statistical machine learning methods can easily work with datasets that are heterogeneous with a mix of continuous, categorical, and binary variables.

To enable the wider adoption of data synthesis, we do not want to be continuously tweaking the parameters of the synthesis models to get them to work. Ideally, a synthesis approach would produce pretty good results all of the time without much labor. That way synthesis can be used by nonexperts in the domain or in the synthesis techniques. The greater the burden, the fewer people will be able to use the methodology.

In the next chapter, we will examine the other side of the ledger: privacy. While we can create high-utility data, it is also important to ensure that the privacy risks are managed. Privacy assurance is an important capability when synthesizing data. In today's regulatory environment, the liability to an organization can be significant if it uses synthetic data as if it is not personal data and then finds out later that the privacy risks were still high.

CHAPTER 6

Identity Disclosure in Synthetic Data

The analysis of privacy risks with synthetic data remains an important topic. In the context of a privacy analysis, we are concerned here with data that pertains to individuals. If the data does not pertain to individuals, then there will be no privacy concerns. For example, if the data pertains to prescriptions or cars, then we would not worry as much about privacy. However, data synthesis is being used extensively to generate data about individuals, and therefore we need to understand the privacy implications.

There is a general belief that synthetic data has negligible privacy risk because there is no unique mapping between the records in the synthetic data and the records in the original data.[1] Reiter noted that "identification of units and their sensitive data from synthetic samples is nearly impossible,"[2] and Taub et al. said that "it is widely understood that thinking of risk within synthetic data in terms of re-identification, which is how many other SDC [statistical disclosure control] methods approach disclosure risk, is not meaningful."[3]

However, in practice, when generating synthetic data it is possible to overfit the synthesis model to the real data, and we have discussed that in earlier chapters of this book. This means that the generated data will look very similar to the original data, hence creating a privacy problem whereby we can map the records in the synthetic

---

1 Jingchen Hu, "Bayesian Estimation of Attribute and Identification Disclosure Risks in Synthetic Data," arXiv, April 2018. *https://arxiv.org/abs/1804.02784.*

2 Jerome P. Reiter, "New Approaches to Data Dissemination: A Glimpse into the Future (?)," *CHANCE* 17, no. 3 (June 2004): 11–15.

3 Jennifer Taub et al., "Differential Correct Attribution Probability for Synthetic Data: An Exploration," in *Privacy in Statistical Databases*, ed. Josep Domingo-Ferrer and Francisco Montes (New York: Springer, 2018), 122–37.

data to individuals in the real world. Therefore, we still need a framework to reason about the privacy risks in synthetic data and methodologies to measure these risks. In practice, we have also seen that the legal teams in many organizations are still looking for concrete evidence that the privacy risks in synthetic data are low, and these teams are not comforted by general assurances from the literature.

In this chapter, we first define more precisely what types of disclosures data synthesis is intended to protect against. We then present a detailed review of how synthetic data is treated in some of the key privacy regulations in the US and the EU. We close the chapter with some ideas on how to start doing a privacy assurance analysis.

Types of Disclosure

This section examines the different types of disclosure of personal information and then shows which ones are relevant from the perspective of data synthesis. We take a pragmatic perspective that attempts to balance the conservative theoretical views sometimes expressed in the literature while acknowledging that many uses of data analysis are beneficial (for example, health research).

Identity Disclosure

Consider the simple dataset in Table 6-1. We have three records with a person's origin and a person's income. For now we assume that this is a real dataset that has not been perturbed.

Let's say that an adversary or hacker is trying to find the record that belongs to someone named Hiroshi. The adversary knows that Hiroshi is in that dataset, and that Hiroshi is Japanese. By using that background knowledge, the adversary would be able to conclude that the first record in the dataset belongs to Hiroshi. In this case, the adversary assigned an identity to the first record. This is called *identity disclosure*.

Table 6-1. An example of a simple dataset to illustrate identity disclosure

Origin	Income
Japanese	$120K
North African	$100K
European	$110K

After matching the first record with Hiroshi, the adversary learns something new about Hiroshi that they did not know beforehand: Hiroshi's income is $120K. This is a material point that we will return to later in this chapter.

We care only about correct assignments of an identity to a record. This is one of the fundamental criteria for considering whether records in synthetic data (or any kind of depersonalized data) have been compromised. For example, if an adversary is unable to find a record that matches Hiroshi's criteria, then disclosure has not occurred. If the adversary assigns the second record to Hiroshi, that would be incorrect, and therefore disclosure has not occurred. Being able to incorrectly assign identities to records is not a problem that we can solve, and therefore the focus is only on correct identity disclosure.

Learning Something New

Another situation is illustrated in Table 6-2. Here, the adversary knows that Hiroshi is in the dataset, that his year of birth is 1959, that he is male, and that he earns $120K. Knowing these four things, the adversary can say with certainty that the first record belongs to Hiroshi. However, the adversary used all of the information in the data to determine Hiroshi's record. In fact, the adversary does not learn anything new by figuring out which record belongs to Hiroshi—the information gain is zero.

Even though the adversary did identify the record that belongs to Hiroshi, when the information gain is zero it is not really a meaningful identity disclosure. In theory, it is not a good thing to be able to assign a record to an individual, but in practice, if the information gain is zero, then there is no point to the identity disclosure. In such cases the risk of harm to the individual is arguably negligible.

Table 6-2. An example of a simple dataset to illustrate identity disclosure where nothing new is learned by the adversary

Year of birth	Gender	Income
1959	Male	$120K
1959	Male	$100K
1959	Female	$120K
1959	Male	$110K
1955	Male	$120K

Therefore, an important criterion to consider when deciding whether a disclosure has occurred is whether there is an information gain from the disclosure.

Attribute Disclosure

Another type of disclosure is *attribute disclosure*, when we learn something new about a group of individuals in the dataset without actually assigning an identity to a record. Consider the data in Table 6-3, which is a health dataset showing ages, genders, and diagnoses.

Let's assume that the adversary knows that Hiroshi is in the data, is male, and was born in 1959. By looking at this dataset the adversary would conclude that Hiroshi is one of the first three records, but it is not possible to know which record specifically belongs to Hiroshi. The adversary can also conclude that Hiroshi has prostate cancer with 100% certainty. In this case, Hiroshi is a member of a group of males born between 1950 and 1959, and all of the members of this group have prostate cancer. Even though the adversary was not able to assign a record to Hiroshi, by virtue of the fact that Hiroshi is a member of that group the adversary could draw conclusions about him and learn something new.

Table 6-3. An example of a simple dataset to illustrate attribute disclosure

Decade of birth	Gender	Diagnosis
1950–1959	Male	Prostate cancer
1950–1959	Male	Prostate cancer
1950–1959	Male	Prostate cancer
1980–1989	Male	Lung cancer
1980–1989	Female	Breast cancer

What the adversary effectively did here is build a model that relates age and gender to diagnosis. It just happens that based on this dataset the model has no uncertainty (i.e., all males born between 1950 and 1959 have a prostate cancer diagnosis).

Let's go one step further and say that an analysis was performed, and the decision tree in Figure 6-1 was built using a machine learning algorithm run on the data and was published in a journal. If we then go through the tree and match Hiroshi's specifics, we see that he is very likely to have prostate cancer according to that model. In this case, we are drawing inferences from the model based on Hiroshi's characteristics.

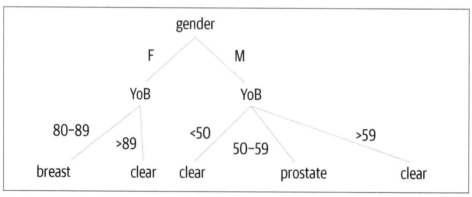

Figure 6-1. A decision tree that was built from an oncology dataset

The model the adversary built was simple, but one can imagine that in other types of datasets these models can be more complex, with additional variables and interactions among the variables. The complexity of the model does not matter for making the main point, though. The adversary engaged in statistics or data analysis. The essence of data analysis is to build models that draw conclusions about groups of individuals with certain characteristics.[4]

The other thing to note here is that the adversary can draw conclusions about individuals who are *not* in the data. If the dataset is representative of the population, then a conclusion can be drawn about all men born between 1950 and 1959 in the population. For example, if Satoshi is a male born in 1955 and is a member of the population that data comes from, then one can reasonably conclude that Satoshi also has prostate cancer. Here, the adversary is learning something new about individuals who are not even in the data, and with high certainty. Again, this is the essence of statistics.

The adversary did not identify the record that belongs to Satoshi because it does not exist in the data. The existence of Satoshi's record in the data, or not, is not relevant here—there is a model that can be used to make inferences without identity disclosure.

We do not want to constrain statistics—that would defeat the whole purpose of AI and data analysis. Therefore, a blanket ban on attribute disclosure would be a bit of an overreach.

Inferential Disclosure

Now let's consider the dataset in Table 6-4. Here, the adversary has the same background information about Hiroshi as in the previous example (he is in the data, male, and born in 1959). The adversary can conclude that Hiroshi has prostate cancer with only 50% certainty. Similarly for Satoshi, the adversary can conclude that he has prostate cancer with 50% certainty, even though Satoshi is not in the data.

Table 6-4. An example of a simple dataset to illustrate attribute disclosure

Decade of birth	Gender	Diagnosis
1950–1959	Male	Prostate cancer
1950–1959	Male	Prostate cancer
1950–1959	Male	Lung cancer
1950–1959	Male	Lung cancer
1980–1989	Female	Breast cancer

The basic point about this being the essence of statistics/data analysis still holds. The difference between this case and the one in Table 6-3 is the level of certainty. In one case a more accurate model has been built. But the record belonging to Hiroshi still

---

4 This assumes that the data is about individuals. If the dataset is about cars, then the models are built for drawing conclusions about types of cars.

cannot be identified, and the only reason we can learn something new about him is because he is a member of a group that has been modeled.

Meaningful Identity Disclosure

We need to specify what data synthesis is going to protect against. We have argued previously that attribute and inferential disclosure are both forms of statistical analysis, and therefore we would not want synthesis to protect against these. We would want models to be built from synthetic data. We would want inferences to be derived from synthetic data. Both of these would pertain to groups with specific characteristics without identifying the records that belong to individuals in that dataset. The reason it is necessary to make this clear is that there have been some regulatory leanings toward requiring methods that render personal information to be nonpersonal to also protect against attribute disclosure and inferences.[5]

We would want synthesis to protect against identity disclosure. This is a necessary but insufficient condition for a disclosure that would be problematic. The second condition is that there is some information gain. If both of these conditions are met, then we call this a *meaningful identity disclosure.*

Learning something new about a group of individuals without identifying any records can potentially be harmful to members of the group. For example, if the adversary learns that members of the group have a stigmatized disease or condition, then this can potentially be harmful. Or perhaps the model that is built from the data can be used in ways that are harmful to members of the group—for example, by discriminating against them when deciding who to give bank loans or insurance to. These are legitimate concerns, but data synthesis will not protect against them. Synthetic data that retains high utility will allow models to be built that retain the original relationships in the data. Therefore, if models from real data can be used in inappropriate ways, so can models from synthetic data. These types of concerns need to be dealt with through ethics reviews on the data and model uses. They are not going to be dealt with through changes to the synthesis process.

Whether particular information is harmful or whether the uses of models from the data are potentially discriminatory may be relative to current cultural norms and the expectations of the public, and these change over time. For example, the question of whether it is appropriate to build biobanks holding people's DNA and use that for research and other secondary purposes was controversial a decade ago but is less so now. Therefore, these assessments are subjective, and a group of individuals who are tasked with making such ethical calls is a known way to manage these kinds of risks.

---

5 For example, see the discussion and references in Khaled El Emam and Cecilia Alvarez, "A Critical Appraisal of the Article 29 Working Party Opinion 05/2014 on Data Anonymization Techniques," *International Data Privacy Law* 5, no. 1 (2015): 73–87.

Defining Information Gain

Now let's consider the concept of information gain from an identity disclosure. The notion of information gain needs to evaluate how unusual the information is. For example, let's say that Aiko has four children. Among Asian Americans, only 10% of women ages 40 to 44 have four or more children. On the other hand, Keiko has only two children, which is quite common among Asian American women in the US (50%). Therefore, learning Aiko's number of children is more informative than Keiko's number of children because Aiko's will stand out within the population of Asian American. In fact, two is the most common number of children among all races in the US, and just guessing that number would have a higher likelihood of getting it right.

An important factor when evaluating meaningful identity disclosure is how usual or common a particular piece of information that we learn about an individual is. Of course, in this analysis we assumed that Aiko's and Keiko's number of children were correct in the synthetic data. In practice, these values will be synthesized as well, and therefore if the numbers generated in the synthetic record are not the same as or close to the true values of the real person, then there will be no or limited information gain.

Bringing It All Together

The decision tree in Figure 6-2 illustrates the types of risks that data synthesis would protect against: meaningful identity disclosure. The risks from other types of disclosure shown here would be managed through ethics reviews and other governance mechanisms, but not through data synthesis.

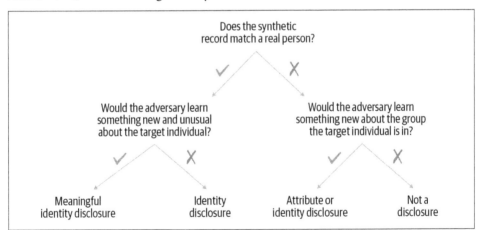

Figure 6-2. Decision tree to determine whether there is a risk of meaningful identity disclosure

In the next section we will examine the legal aspects of managing meaningful identity disclosure through data synthesis

Unique Matches

In many datasets the real data sample (the "real sample") is a subsample from some population. This real sample may have records that match the synthetic dataset (the "synthetic sample"). This matching happens on *quasi-identifiers*, which are the subset of variables that an adversary can know about real people in the population. If an adversary is able to match a synthetic record with a person in the population, then this is an identity disclosure. The concept is illustrated in Figure 6-3.

One simple way to screen the synthesized data for records that can potentially be identifying is to identify and remove unique records in the real sample that can be matched with a unique record in the synthetic sample, with the matching done on the quasi-identifiers. For example, if there was only one 50-year-old male (the age and gender variables are the quasi-identifiers) in the real sample and only one 50-year-old male in the synthetic sample, then these two records match with certainty. The next question is whether that 50-year-old male in the real sample can be matched with someone in the population with a high probability.

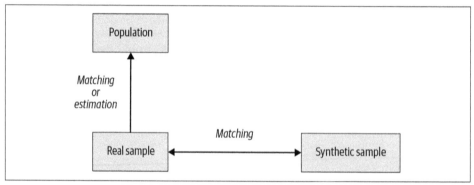

Figure 6-3. The process of matching a synthetic record to a real person

The risk of identification is a function of individuals in the population, and because most real datasets represent samples from that population, this means that records that are unique in the real data are not necessarily unique in the population. For example, if there are ten 50-year-old males in the population, then there is a 1:10 chance that the real record can be correctly matched to the right individual. A very conservative approach would be to assume that if the record is unique in the real sample, then it will match correctly and with certainty with a person in the population. And if that record in turn matches a unique record in the synthetic sample, then that establishes a one-to-one mapping between the synthetic sample and an individual.

In our example from the previous chapter with using decision trees for synthesis on the hospital discharge data, we found that 4% of the records were unique in the synthetic data and were also unique in the real dataset. Therefore, these records can be removed from the synthetic dataset as a privacy protection measure.

This approach is really quite conservative and can be considered a simple first step to empirically evaluating the identity disclosure risks in a synthetic dataset. More sophisticated methods can be applied to statistically estimate the probability of matching a synthetic record to a real person, accounting for different attack methods that an adversary can use.

How Privacy Law Impacts the Creation and Use of Synthetic Data

Synthetic data offers a compelling solution to data sharing and data-access barriers—one that promotes greater scientific and commercial research while protecting individual privacy.[6]

An original set of real personal information is used in the creation and evaluation of a synthetic dataset. A synthetic dataset is generated from a real dataset. The synthetic dataset has the same statistical properties as the real data. But it is not real data. It is not data about or related to any real individual person or people. A single record in a synthetic dataset does not correspond to an individual or record in the real dataset. And to ensure that the resulting synthetic dataset does not inadvertently reveal information about a real person from the original dataset, a privacy assurance process evaluates the privacy risk of the synthetic data—comparing the real and the synthetic data to assess and remove any such risk.

Synthetic data differs from what is traditionally thought of as the de-identification of data. De-identification is a means of altering a dataset to remove, mask, or transform direct and indirect identifiers. But the de-identified data is still real data related to real individuals. It has just made it less likely that any individual in the record can be identified from the data. Depending on the method and strength of the de-identification, it can be an excellent risk-mitigation measure. But depending on the applicable laws, it may still be treated as personal information, and there still can be significant regulatory overhead. Contracts with data recipients may need to be in place, security precautions must be taken, and distribution may need to be limited.

---

6 This section of the chapter is for informational purposes only and is not intended to provide, nor shall it be construed as providing, any any legal opinion or conclusion, does not constitute legal advice, and is not a substitute for obtaining professional legal counsel from a qualified attorney on your specific matter. The material here was prepared by Mike Hintze from the firm Hintze Law.

Synthetic data is different. It is not real data related to real people. There is no link between a synthetic dataset and records in the original (real) dataset. If done properly, the creation of synthetic data should result in a dataset that cannot be reverse engineered to reveal identities of real people or information specific to a real person.[7] For any given synthetic dataset, this conclusion is testable and verifiable through statistical analysis. Thus, a properly created and verified synthetic dataset that is not constrained by privacy law can be freely distributed (including publicly released) and used broadly for analysis and research.

But that does not mean that privacy laws are irrelevant. Because synthetic data must start with a real dataset, the handling and use of that real dataset is still likely to be regulated by privacy law.

If an organization does not have the capability and expertise to create synthetic data in-house, it may need to share the original (real) dataset with a service provider to create the synthetic data. That sharing is also likely to be subject to privacy law.

This section addresses how the creation and use of synthetic data is regulated under three key privacy laws: the European General Data Protection Regulation (GDPR),[8] the California Consumer Privacy Act (CCPA),[9] and the US Health Insurance Portability and Accountability Act (HIPAA).[10]

For each of these privacy laws, this chapter will examine three key questions:

- Is the use of the original (real) dataset to generate and/or evaluate a synthetic dataset restricted or regulated under the law?

- Is sharing the original dataset with a third-party service provider to generate the synthetic dataset restricted or regulated under the law?

- Does the law regulate or otherwise affect (if at all) the resulting synthetic dataset?

In sum, while these laws regulate or potentially regulate the generation and evaluation of synthetic data, as well as the sharing of the original dataset with third-party service

---

7 This conclusion holds true even if the person using the synthetic dataset has or could gain access to the original dataset. That would not occur in most cases, since the key objective of creating synthetic data is to enable the benefits of data use and analysis without giving access to real, personal data. Nevertheless, it may be worthwhile to have in place additional safeguards such as strong access controls on the original dataset, and contractual prohibitions on any attempts to reverse engineer or link the synthetic data to the original data.

8 Regulation (EU) 2016/679 of the European Parliament and of the Council of 27 April 2016 on the protection of natural persons with regard to the processing of personal data and on the free movement of such data, and repealing Directive 95/46/EC (General Data Protection Regulation), 2016 O.J. (L 119) 1 (hereinafter "GDPR").

9 California Consumer Privacy Act of 2018, Cal. Civ. Code §§1798.100-1798.199 (hereinafter "CCPA").

10 Health Insurance Portability and Accountability Act of 1996, Pub. L. 104-191 (hereinafter "HIPAA"); Standards for Privacy of Individually Identifiable Health Information, 45 C.F.R. Parts 160 and 164 (hereinafter "HIPAA Privacy Rule").

providers, none pose a significant barrier to doing so. Sharing the original data with a service provider is permitted as long as an appropriate contract is in place and the parties adhere to its requirements. And once a fully synthetic dataset is created, this data should be seen as falling outside the scope of these laws, and therefore not subject to any restrictions on the subsequent use or dissemination of the data (including making the data publicly available).

We conclude the section with an analysis of an opinion on what makes information identifiable, published by an advisory body of European regulators (the Article 29 Working Party). We provide a pragmatic interpretation of that opinion and explain how that can be applied to synthetic data.

Issues Under the GDPR

Here we address some common questions regarding how the GDPR applies to synthetic data generation and use.

Is the use of the original (real) dataset to generate and/or evaluate a synthetic dataset restricted or regulated under the GDPR?

Yes. The GDPR regulates any "processing" of personal data. And "processing" is defined as "any operation or set of operations which is performed on personal data or on sets of personal data, whether or not by automated means."[11] Because the generation of synthetic data involves the processing of a real dataset, the obligations that the GDPR imposes on the processing of personal data apply to this operation.

In particular, the GDPR requires there to be a "legal basis" to process personal data. Thus, to the extent that the original dataset includes personal data, the use of that dataset to generate or evaluate a synthetic dataset requires a legal basis. There are several legal bases available under the GDPR. One well-known legal basis is the consent of the individual.

But obtaining consent from every individual contained in a dataset in order to develop a synthetic dataset will often be impractical or impossible. Further, seeking consent from data subjects to process data in order to create synthetic data (and excluding the data from those individuals who do not consent) could undermine the statistical validity of the generated synthetic data because there is significant evidence of consent bias.[12]

---

11 GDPR Art. 4(2).

12 See Khaled El Emam et al., "A Review of Evidence on Consent Bias in Research," *The American Journal of Bioethics* 13, no. 4 (2013): 42–44. *https://oreil.ly/5x5kg*; Michelle E. Kho et al., "Written Informed Consent and Selection Bias in Observational Studies Using Medical Records: Systematic Review," *BMJ* 338:b866 (March 2009). *https://doi.org/10.1136/bmj.b866.*

Instead, a more practical and appropriate legal basis will be "legitimate interests." This legal basis applies when the legitimate interests of the data controller or a third party outweigh the interests or rights of the data subject. Inherent in the use of this legal basis is a balancing test. In this context, one must consider the interest in processing personal data in order to create a synthetic dataset and weigh that interest against the risks to the data subject.

An organization that has a need or desire to use data for a purpose that a synthetic dataset can help achieve, or that wishes to advance beneficial research while reducing the organization's legal risk and protecting the privacy of individuals, will have a very strong interest in the creation of a synthetic dataset that can be used for research in lieu of using real data. On the other side of the equation, assuming the creation of synthetic data is done in a secure environment, there is little or no risk to the data subject. On the contrary, the data subject has an interest in the creation of the synthetic data because it eliminates the risk inherent in sharing and using the original (real) dataset for a research purpose when the synthetic data can be used instead. Thus, the legitimate interests balancing test comes out strongly in favor of using the personal data to create the synthetic dataset.

Beyond the need to establish a legal basis for processing, the GDPR includes a number of additional obligations relating to the collection, use, and disclosure of personal data—which apply in this scenario just as they apply to any processing of personal data. Thus, the organization handling the original dataset must ensure that the personal data is kept secure and protected from unauthorized access or disclosure.[13] The organization must meet its notice and transparency obligations, so it may be prudent to ensure that the applicable privacy notice(s) contemplate and disclose the types of processing that are involved in the creation and testing of synthetic datasets.[14] And the organization must maintain records of its processing activities; here too the organization should simply make sure that this use of data to create synthetic data is in some way reflected in those records.

However, these are obligations the organization must meet with respect to its collection and processing of the original dataset in any event, whether or not that set is used in the generation of synthetic data. The use of personal data to create synthetic data will, at most, have a modest impact on how the organization meets those

---

13 GDPR Art. 32 ("Taking into account the state of the art, the costs of implementation and the nature, scope, context and purposes of processing as well as the risk of varying likelihood and severity for the rights and freedoms of natural persons, the controller and the processor shall implement appropriate technical and organisational measures to ensure a level of security appropriate to the risk").

14 GDPR Art. 13(1) ("the controller shall, at the time when personal data are obtained, provide the data subject with all of the following information… (c) the purposes of the processing for which the personal data are intended").

obligations. But it does not create fundamentally new obligations, nor does it significantly increase the burden or difficulty of meeting these existing obligations.

Is sharing the original dataset with a third-party service provider to generate the synthetic dataset restricted or regulated under the GDPR?

Under the GDPR, any entity processing personal data will be either a "data controller" or a "data processor." A data controller is an entity that "alone or jointly with others, determines the purposes and means of the processing of personal data." A data processor is an entity that processes personal data on behalf of, and at the direction of, the controller. For the purposes of this discussion, we can assume that the owner of the dataset is the data controller, and the service provider that the controller hires to generate synthetic data from that original dataset is a data processor.

A data controller can provide personal data to a data processor as necessary to enable the data processor to perform a service at the direction of and on behalf of the data controller. So, sharing an original dataset with a third-party service provider to generate a synthetic dataset is permitted under the GDPR. However, the GDPR imposes certain restrictions on that data sharing and on the parties involved.

A controller that wishes to share personal data with a processor has a duty of care in selecting a processor that can provide "sufficient guarantees" that it will process personal data in compliance with the requirements of the GDPR and will protect the rights of the data subject(s).

The GDPR further requires that there be a contract between the controller and the processor that obligates the processor to do the following:

- Process the personal data "only on documented instructions from the controller"
- Ensure that each person processing the personal data is subject to a duty of confidentiality with respect to the data
- Implement and maintain reasonable security procedures and practices to protect personal data
- Engage a subcontractor only pursuant to a written contract that passes through the data protection requirements and only with the general or specific prior consent of the controller[15]

---

15 GDPR Art. 28(2), (3)(d), and (4). "General" consent for the processor to use subcontractors can be provided in advance, including as part of the contract, so long as the processor informs the controller of any addition of replacement of subcontractors, and gives the controller the opportunity to object.

- Assist the controller in enabling data subjects to exercise their rights under the GDPR[16]

- Assist the controller as needed to meet the controller's obligations with respect to data security, notification of data breaches, risk assessments, and consultation with regulators

- Delete or return all personal data to the controller at the completion of the service(s)—unless retention is required by law

- Provide to the controller, upon request, "all information necessary to demonstrate compliance with [the processor's] obligations…and allow for and contribute to audits, including inspections, conducted by the controller or another auditor mandated by the controller"

As long as the contract with the required terms for data processors is in place, and those measures are adhered to, providing the original dataset to a service provider in order to create a synthetic dataset will be permissible under the GDPR.

Does the GDPR regulate or otherwise affect (if at all) the resulting synthetic dataset?

Once the synthetic dataset has been generated, any regulation of that dataset under the GDPR depends on whether it can be considered "personal data."

The GDPR defines "personal data" as follows:

> Any information relating to an identified or identifiable natural person ("data subject"); an identifiable natural person is one who can be identified, directly or indirectly, in particular by reference to an identifier such as a name, an identification number, location data, an online identifier or to one or more factors specific to the physical, physiological, genetic, mental, economic, cultural or social identity of that natural person.[17]

Synthetic data is not real data about a person. Although it is based on a real dataset, a single record in a synthetic dataset does not correspond to an individual or record in the original (real) dataset. Thus, a record in a synthetic dataset does not relate to an actual natural person. It does not include an identifier that corresponds to an actual natural person. It does not reference the physical, physiological, genetic, mental, economic, cultural, or social identity of an actual natural person. In short, a fully synthetic dataset does not meet the GDPR definition of "personal data." As such, it is

---

16 GDPR Art. 28(3)(e). In cases where a data processor holds personal data for a relatively short period of time, as would be the case here, where the original dataset containing personal data is processed by the service provider for only as long as is required to create and test the synthetic dataset, it is unlikely that this obligation to assist the data controller with requests from data subjects (such as requests to access or delete data) would apply in a significant way.

17 GDPR Art. 4(1).

outside the scope of the GDPR. It therefore can be used and distributed, including being made publicly available, without restriction.

Issues Under the CCPA

Here we address some common questions regarding how the CCPA applies to synthetic data generation and use.

Is the use of the original (real) dataset to generate and/or evaluate a synthetic dataset restricted or regulated under the CCPA?

Unlike the GDPR, the CCPA does not require the establishment of a legal basis for the processing of personal information. Nor does it place significant restrictions on a company's collection or internal use of personal information. Instead, it is largely focused on regulating the "sales" of personal information, which is defined broadly to cover many transfers of personal information in a commercial context.

As a result, the act of using an existing dataset to create a synthetic dataset is not specifically regulated by the CCPA. Thus, the CCPA does not prevent or restrict the use of personal information to generate and/or evaluate a synthetic dataset.

Instead, as with the GDPR, such data use may be subject to some CCPA obligations, such as providing notice of how the personal information is used, which will apply to the organization whether or not it uses the data to generate synthetic data.

Is sharing the original dataset with a third-party service provider to generate the synthetic dataset restricted or regulated under the CCPA?

As noted previously, the CCPA regulates the "sale" of personal information, and sales are defined very broadly. However, certain transfers of personal information to a "service provider" are exempt from the definition of "sale."[18] Specifically, if personal data is transferred by a business to a service provider, that transfer will not be regulated as a sale under the CCPA as long as the following requirements are met:

- The business has provided notice that personal information will be shared with service providers
- The service provider does not collect, use, sell, or disclose the personal data for any purpose other than as necessary to provide the service(s) on behalf of the business
- There is a written contract between the business and the service provider that specifies the service provider is prohibited from retaining, using, selling, or

---

18 Note that virtually every organization shares some data with a service provider from time to time, so the organization's privacy notice should already have such a disclosure.

disclosing the personal information for any purpose other than performing the services specified in the contract on behalf of the business

Thus, as long as these criteria are met, including having a contract in place between the business and the service provider,[19] a business subject to the CCPA can share a dataset containing personal information with a service provider that uses it to generate synthetic data on behalf of that business.

Does the CCPA regulate or otherwise affect (if at all) the resulting synthetic dataset?

The CCPA defines "personal information" as any information "that identifies, relates to, describes, is reasonably capable of being associated with, or could reasonably be linked, directly or indirectly, with a particular consumer or household." While this is a very broad definition of personal information, it should not include synthetic data. As noted previously, synthetic data is not real data that relates to a real person. When a synthetic dataset is created using a real dataset, there is no association between an individual record in a real set and an individual record in the resulting synthetic dataset. Thus, records in a synthetic set should not be seen as being associated, linked, or related to a particular real consumer or household.

Further, the CCPA definition of personal information specifies that it does not include aggregate consumer information. And "aggregate consumer information" is defined as "information that relates to a group or category of consumers, from which individual consumer identities have been removed, that is not linked or reasonably linkable to any consumer or household, including via a device." Thus, although a synthetic dataset could be seen as applying to a group or category of consumers, the exclusion for aggregate data gives additional weight to the conclusion that a synthetic dataset is not covered by the CCPA definition of personal information.

Thus, because synthetic data is not "personal information" under the CCPA, it is not subject to the requirements of the CCPA. It can therefore be freely used and distributed—even sold—without restriction under the CCPA.

Issues Under HIPAA

Here we address some common questions regarding the application of HIPAA to synthetic data generation and use.

---

19 Some of the contract terms required under the CCPA for service providers are similar, but not identical, to the contract terms required under the GDPR for data processors. However, it is possible, and often prudent, to create terms that meet both, so that a single contract works for both CCPA and GDPR purposes.

Is the use of the original (real) dataset to generate and/or evaluate a synthetic dataset restricted or regulated under HIPAA?

HIPAA permits the use of protected health information (PHI) to create a synthetic dataset. The HIPAA Privacy Rule specifies certain uses of PHI that are permitted without the authorization of the individual and without providing the individual the opportunity to agree or object.

One such permitted use is described as follows:

> Uses and disclosures to create de-identified information. A covered entity may use protected health information to create information that is not individually identifiable health information or disclose protected health information only to a business associate for such purpose.[20]

That permitted use is reinforced in a different section of the HIPAA Privacy Rule that describes health care operations as another permitted use. Health care operations is defined to include "general administrative activities of the entity, including, but not limited to…creating de-identified health information or a limited data set."[21]

The creation of a synthetic dataset is distinct from what has traditionally been thought of as de-identification. De-identification typically involves removing, masking, or transforming direct and indirect identifiers within a record. But the resulting de-identified dataset is generally thought of as an altered version of the original dataset in which there remains some correlation between records in the original dataset and records in the de-identified dataset. By contrast, synthetic data is the creation of a completely new dataset, and while the synthetic dataset is statistically similar to the original (real) dataset, there is no direct correlation between records in the original dataset and those in the synthetic dataset.

Nevertheless, although both of these sections of the HIPAA Privacy Rule reference de-identification, both should be interpreted broadly enough to include the creation of synthetic data as a permitted use of PHI. In the first quoted section, the key phrase is "to create information that is not individually identifiable health information," which is precisely what is happening when PHI is used to create synthetic data because synthetic data is not individually identifiable data (more on that following). And in describing de-identification in that way, the HIPAA Privacy Rule strongly indicates that the concept of de-identification in HIPAA is broad enough to encompass any action that uses PHI to create a dataset that does not contain individually identifiable information.

---

20 HIPAA Privacy Rule § 164.502(d)(1).

21 A "limited data set" is a dataset that has had certain identifiers removed but that does not meet the HIPAA standard for fully de-identified information. See HIPAA Privacy Rule § 164.514(e)(2).

Additionally, the part of the "health care operations" definition that includes "creating de-identified health information or a limited data set" is preceded by the phrase "including, but not limited to." So, it is easy to conclude that a very similar type of operation that results in strong privacy protections for individuals is also included in that category of permitted uses. Further, with respect to both sections, given that synthetic data will almost always be even more privacy-protecting than de-identified data, there is no policy reason why these aspects of the HIPAA Privacy Rule should be interpreted narrowly or that HIPAA should treat the creation of synthetic data less favorably than the use of PHI to create a de-identified dataset.

Thus, viewing the creation of synthetic data as a permitted use of PHI under the HIPAA Privacy Rule is both a sensible and sound conclusion.

Is sharing the original dataset with a third-party service provider to generate the synthetic dataset restricted or regulated under HIPAA?

Under HIPAA, a covered entity is permitted to share PHI with another entity providing a service on behalf of that covered entity. Such a service provider is called a "business associate" of the covered entity.

There must be a contract or similar arrangement in place between a covered entity and the business associate. The contract must specify the nature of the service for which the PHI is shared, describe the permitted and required uses of protected health information by the business associate, provide assurances that the business associate will appropriately protect the privacy and security of the PHI, and meet certain other requirements.[22] Thus, a contract for the creation of synthetic data should state that the service provider may use PHI to generate and evaluate one or more synthetic datasets.[23] In addition to the contractual terms, business associates are directly subject to the HIPAA Security Rule and certain aspects of the HIPAA Privacy Rule.

Thus, a service provider that receives PHI from a HIPAA-covered entity for the purpose of creating synthetic data is likely to be considered a business associate of the covered entity. As long as there is an appropriate contract in place that meets the requirements of a business associate agreement under the HIPAA Privacy Rule, and the service provider meets its other obligations under the rule, the sharing of PHI with the service provider is allowed.

---

22 Guidance from the US Department of Health and Human Services on the required elements of a business associate agreement, as well as sample contractual language, is available at *https://oreil.ly/53Ef0*.

23 If the service provider is performing a broader range of services, and the creation of synthetic data is an inherent part of those services, the parties could argue that it is permitted even if the contract does not explicitly state that. But for the avoidance of doubt, any time a covered entity is sharing data containing PHI with a service provider to create a synthetic dataset, the parties should explicitly reference synthetic data creation in the contract as a permitted use of the PHI.

Does HIPAA regulate or otherwise affect (if at all) the resulting synthetic dataset?

Synthetic data falls outside the scope of HIPAA. HIPAA regulates "individually identifiable health information" and "protected health information." "Individually identifiable health information" is information created or received by a covered entity, relating to the physical or mental health or condition of an individual, the provision of healthcare to an individual, or the payment for the provision of healthcare to an individual, where that information either identifies the individual or for which there is a reasonable basis to believe the information can be used to identify the individual. "Protected health information" is roughly the same; it is defined as "individually identifiable health information," subject to a few minor exclusions for certain educational records and employment records.

Because synthetic data is not "real" data related to actual individuals, synthetic data does not identify any individual, nor can it reasonably be used to identify an individual. Synthetic data is therefore outside the scope of HIPAA and not subject to the requirements of the HIPAA rules. It can therefore be freely used for secondary analysis, shared for research purposes, or made publicly available without restriction.

Article 29 Working Party Opinion

The Article 29 Working Party (now the European Data Protection Board) published an influential opinion in 2014 on anonymization.[24] Although our focus here is not on anonymization, that opinion does describe European regulators' views on when information no longer becomes identifiable.[25] As well as being influential, the opinion has been critiqued on multiple dimensions.[26] Nevertheless, in the following sections we describe the criteria from this opinion for information to be non-identifiable, present our interpretation of these criteria, and explain how synthetic data would meet these criteria. At the end, we make the case that synthetic data can meet the three criteria and therefore would be considered nonpersonal information under this opinion.

The three criteria, their interpretations, and an assessment of synthetic data on each criterion are below.

---

24 The Article 29 Working Party is an advisory body made up of representatives from the European data protection authorities, the European Data Protection Supervisor, and the European Commission. From time to time it has published opinions interpreting and clarifying various aspects of data protection regulation.

25 Article 29 Data Protection Working Party, "Opinion 05/2014 on Anonymisation Techniques," April 2014. *https://www.pdpjournals.com/docs/88197.pdf.*

26 Khaled El Emam and Cecilia Alvarez, "A Critical Appraisal of the Article 29 Working Party Opinion 05/2014 on Data Anonymization Techniques," *International Data Privacy Law* 5, no. 1 (2015): 73–87.

Singling out

Singling out is defined as the ability to isolate some or all of the records that identify an individual in a dataset. This can be interpreted in two ways. The first is that there should be no individuals in the dataset that are also unique in the population (on the quasi-identifiers). The second is that there should not be a correct mapping between a record in the dataset and a real person.

In the case of synthetic data, there would be no unique synthetic records that map to unique real records, and hence by definition there would not be a mapping to a unique individual in the population. With respect to the second interpretation, a key premise of synthetic data is that there is no one-to-one mapping between synthetic records and individuals, and therefore this interpretation should also be met in practice.

Linkability

Linkability is the ability to link at least two records concerning the same data subject or a group of data subjects. One interpretation of this is that linkability applies to linking records that belong to the same person in the same database. This is essentially a ban on longitudinal data.[27] That interpretation has been criticized because it would have a significant negative impact on, for example, health research.

Another interpretation is that this criterion bans assigning individuals to groups, which essentially prohibits building statistical models from data (since models are based on detecting group patterns across individuals). Again, in the real world such an interpretation would halt many secondary uses of data.

Therefore, the interpretation that is generally adopted is that individuals cannot be linked across databases. This criterion is met by definition because the likelihood of successfully linking synthetic records in one database with real records in another database is going to be very low.

Inference

Inference is defined as the possibility of deducing with a high likelihood the value of an attribute from the values of a set of other attributes. One interpretation of this criterion is that it is a ban on statistics and model building, which is likely not the intent here because that would also limit the uses of aggregate/summary statistics from data involving more than one variable.

Therefore, the general interpretation is that it should not be possible to make inferences that are specific to individuals. However, inferences that pertain to groups of

---

27 Khaled El Emam and Cecilia Alvarez, "A Critical Appraisal of the Article 29 Working Party Opinion 05/2014 on Data Anonymization Techniques," *International Data Privacy Law* 5, no. 1 (2015): 73–87.

individuals (which is the essence of model building) would not fall within its scope. Since synthetic data does not have records that pertain to real individuals, any individual inferences would not be about specific individuals. In practice, the inferences are mostly about groups of individuals. In particular, our definition of meaningful identity disclosure would limit the information gain about specific individuals, which supports meeting this criterion.

Closing comments on the Article 29 opinion

The previous sections are a pragmatic interpretation of the three criteria in the Article 29 Working Party opinion. Synthetic data would meet these criteria in a relatively straightforward manner because it would not be matched to unique individuals, records cannot be linked across datasets, and individual-level inferences would not be possible.

Also note that some of the more general interpretations of these criteria are intended to limit risks from misuses of data and AIML models, which are best addressed through governance mechanisms and ethics reviews rather than through data transformation or generation methods.

Summary

Synthetic data is intended to protect against meaningful identity disclosure. That is, it protects against when a synthetic record is associated with a real person, and an adversary can learn something new and unusual about the target individual. Synthetic data therefore offers the promise of extracting great value from data without the privacy risk and regulatory compliance costs associated with the use of personal data or even de-identified data.

The creation of synthetic data involves the processing of a real dataset containing personal information, so the initial creation and testing of a synthetic dataset likely will fall within the scope of privacy law. But most privacy laws allow such use, subject to certain requirements such as keeping the original dataset secure and ensuring that applicable privacy notices do not preclude such use. But these are typically compliance measures that the owner of the original dataset will need to undertake in any event.

Likewise, most privacy laws allow the original dataset to be shared with third-party service providers. So data owners can provide an original dataset to a service provider that will use the data to create the synthetic data on behalf of the data owner, as long as certain data protection measures are taken. Those measures include implementing security safeguards and ensuring that an appropriate contract is in place.

And once the synthetic data is created, because it is not real data relating to real individuals, it will fall outside the scope of privacy law. It can therefore be freely used and distributed for research and other purposes.

This chapter examined three key privacy laws—Europe's GDPR, California's CCPA, and the US federal HIPAA law. Although these laws take different approaches to regulating data protection, and their details differ significantly, the conclusions regarding the creation, distribution, and use of synthetic data are similar for each. And although there can be wide variation in privacy laws across jurisdictions and sectors, they all tend to rely on similar principles and make allowances for uses of personal information that can create great social and individual benefit so long as the risks are appropriately managed. Thus, although these questions must be examined for any privacy law to which the relevant parties are subject, it is likely that the conclusions will be similar.

CHAPTER 7

Practical Data Synthesis

Real data is messy. When data has been cleaned up and heavily curated, then data synthesis methods (and for that matter any data analysis methods) become much easier. But the actual requirement in practice is to synthesize data that has not been curated.

This chapter presents a number of pragmatic considerations for handling real-world data based on our experiences delivering synthetic datasets and synthetic data generation technology. While our list is not comprehensive, it covers some of the more common issues that will be encountered. We highlight the challenges as well as provide some suggestions for addressing them.

At this point, we do not make explicit assumptions about the scale of the data that will be synthesized. For example, some datasets, such as financial transactions or insurance claims, can have a few variables (tens or maybe even hundreds) but a very large number of records. Other datasets can have few individuals covered but a large number of variables (thousands or tens of thousands). These narrow and deep versus wide and shallow datasets present different challenges when processing them for data synthesis. In some cases, the challenges can be handled manually, and in other cases full automation is a necessity.

Managing Data Complexity

The first set of items that we want to cover pertains to how to manage data complexity. If you work with data then you are used to handling data challenges. In the context of synthesis there are some additional considerations.

For Every Pre-Processing Step There Is a Post-Processing Step

The data users expect their synthetic data to have the same structure as the real data. This means that the variable names have to be the same, the field types need to be the same, and the data model for the real data has to be maintained in the synthetic data. However, the data synthesis methods that we discussed need inputs in a certain format. The data may have to be scaled to be within a certain range (say, 0 to 1) and all of the data tables joined to create a single data frame. All such data pre-processing steps must be undone during the post-processing step.

We are making a distinction between data preparation and data pre-processing. Data preparation can be performed by the data provider. For example, if there are multiple datasets that are being pooled together, a certain amount of data harmonization has to be performed beforehand. Data preparation needs to be performed, typically, for any kind of data analysis work and not just for data synthesis. This would similarly be the case when different datasets are being linked to create an integrated dataset to work with. Such data integration happens during the preparation stage by the data providers.

Data shaping, on the other hand, is a synthesis pre-processing step. For example, data with attribute-value pairs are often difficult to work with in standard statistical analysis tools, and therefore this data will need to be reshaped into a more common tabular format. The synthesis pre-processing is part of the methodology and technology, and will be closely tied to the methods used for data synthesis.

Field Types

The pre-processing of datasets for synthesis will depend largely on the type of fields. For example, a continuous variable is pre-processed quite differently than a nominal variable. For large datasets with hundreds or thousands of variables it is not practical to do this classification manually. It is therefore important to be able to autoclassify field types to determine in an efficient manner the best way to pre-process and post-process each variable.

While this seems like a trivial thing to do, when there is no metadata, and domain knowledge is limited, it is not trivial at all.

The Need for Rules

It is quite common that datasets have deterministic relationships. Examples of these are calculated fields where the inputs are other fields, such as BMI (body mass index), which is calculated from height and weight. This relationship is deterministic. But the synthesis methods are mostly stochastic and will have some error in them when synthesized. It is better to detect these deterministic relationships in advance and remove the calculated fields before synthesis. Then after the covariates are synthesized, these derived values are calculated and inserted into the synthetic data.

Calculated fields show up in questionnaires and surveys—for example, where an index score is computed from the responses to the questions. Deterministically derived fields can be interpretations from laboratory results based on some rules. For example, if a lab result exceeds a threshold, then it is considered not normal.

In large datasets, manually documenting every calculated field can be time-consuming. In such cases, methods are needed to automatically detect such rules in the dataset and perform the necessary pre-processing and post-processing steps.

Not All Fields Have to Be Synthesized

There will almost always be at least one field that is a unique identifier. This could be a Social Security number, for example, that is used to identify every individual in the dataset. Or it can be a hospital identifier or a subject ID in a clinical trial dataset. For more complex datasets there will be more than one—for example, an identifier for every visit that the person makes to a hospital or a bank, and a unique transaction identifier for every drug that is dispensed from the pharmacy or item sold at the store.

The methods we have described thus far would not apply to unique identifiers. As a first step, it will be necessary to detect these unique identifiers in the original dataset. In many instances that is relatively straightforward to do because these fields will have the same number of values as there are records. But that is not always the case. Sometimes we see orphan records that do not have unique identifiers. A decision needs to be made about the orphan records. From a data synthesis perspective they can be synthesized, but if the unique identifiers link multiple sources of information, then the correlations with other information about these individuals will not be accounted for.

Sometimes there are compound unique identifiers. These are more challenging to detect, and a good understanding of the data model is needed to find them. A compound identifier is when more than one field makes up the unique identifier.

Once the unique identifiers are found, they are then pseudonymized in the synthetic data. There are multiple methods for pseudonymization. Cryptographic techniques can be used for that purpose (e.g., encryption or hashing), or the unique identifiers can be replaced by random values that are a one-to-one mapping to the original identifiers.

It is recommended that you prepend a special character (such as an "s_") to the synthetic pseudonymized values. This will ensure that the data users do not mistake the synthetic data for real data. Knowing the provenance of the dataset is important. However, adding an "s_" at the beginning of the pseudonymized values may not work if the value is an integer and we want to maintain field types. Therefore, other mechanisms may need to be used.

Synthesizing Dates

The synthesis of dates needs special consideration. There are at least two types of dates. We will call them demographic dates (date of birth, date of death, date of marriage) where the exact date (or an approximation of it) is important. And there are event dates where the interval between them is the most important.

Demographic dates can be represented as an integer and synthesized using the traditional approach for integers. For example, demographic dates can be treated as the number of days since January 1, 1990.

For event dates, it is easiest to convert them to relative dates. This means that an anchor date that is specific to the individual (and that exists for all individuals in the data) is selected, and all dates are converted to days since that anchor. For example, in a clinical trial dataset it can be the date of randomization or date of screening. In an oncology dataset it can be the date of diagnosis. For a financial services dataset it can be the date the individual became a client or opened an account. Then the relative dates can be synthesized.

When there are multiple related dates and no obvious anchor to use, it is important to maintain the relationships among the dates. For example, the synthesized dataset should not have a date of discharge that occurs before a date of admission. In such a case, a length of stay can be calculated and the admission date is synthesized. Then the discharge date is computed *after* synthesis using the synthesized length of stay and admission date. Caution is needed to manage these temporal relationships.

Alternatively, we can add an independent random offset to each patient's dates. That way the relative intervals are maintained, but no exact dates are retained.

In datasets with a large number of events, there are a few ways to deal with the temporal nature of the data. One approach is to "flatten" the data and have all of the events appear as columns. This works well when all the individuals in the dataset will have the same series of events. For example, this happens in clinical trials in which the visits are preplanned or in oncology datasets in which the treatment plans have a predetermined schedule. With such a flattened dataset, commonly used cross-sectional data synthesis techniques can be applied. In other cases where the data is more transactional, more sophisticated methods that account for the temporal dependencies would be needed for accurate data synthesis.

Synthesizing Geography

A typical example of a geographic variable is a zip code or a postal code. Since these are nominal variables in a dataset, they can be treated as other nominal variables and synthesized.

If location is captured by longitude and latitude, there is more complexity because the synthesized locations cannot be, for example, in the middle of the ocean or in a mine. Therefore, again, auxiliary information is needed to handle location.

In practice, more traditional data protection methods, such as generalization or perturbation of locations, are used here. Exact location fields cannot be treated in the same manner as other fields in the dataset.

Lookup Fields and Tables

Some datasets will have lookup fields. This is when the value in a field is a key to look up the true value in a different table. In general this is not a problem because the synthesis process can work equally well on the lookup values instead of the actual values. However, in such cases the lookup tables themselves should not be synthesized. The detection and carving out of these tables is an important step in pre-processing.

Missing Data and Other Data Characteristics

Real data will have missing values. These are generally not a problem for synthesis because the synthesis process will just replicate the missingness patterns in the original data. In some cases, the data synthesis analysts will try to impute the missing values before synthesis, and then synthesize from a complete dataset. This can also be performed as long as the imputation is performed reliably; the only caveat is that this adds significantly to the complexity of the synthesis project, and end-user data analysts will likely want to have control of the imputation process.

The general assumption is that other data quality issues have been dealt with prior to the synthesis process. If not, then these data quality issues will be reflected in the synthetic data—data synthesis does not clean dirty data. For example, if the coding scheme used in a variable is not applied consistently (e.g., it was entered manually and has errors, or different versions of the same coding dictionary were used over time with no version indicator), then that characteristic will be reflected in the synthetic data.

Under the general scheme that we have described in this book, text fields cannot be synthesized. While there is a whole body of work on the synthesis of text, we have not addressed that here. Therefore, we are assuming that text fields will be deleted from the synthesized datasets for the time being.

Datasets that consist of long sequences, such as genomic data, have a specialized set of techniques for their synthesis, similar to text. Long sequences also show up in movement trajectories (e.g., cars, people, and trucks). Trajectories have location and temporal complexities added to them—in that sense every event in the sequence has a number of attributes associated with it. The methods we have discussed in this book will not address these types of data, and synthesizing this kind of information represents areas of ongoing research.

Partial Synthesis

Some datasets are quite complex, and the synthesis process needs to maintain a large amount of information between the entities. When these entities are individual records rather than tables, the complexity can be significant. For such datasets the solution is to create a partially synthetic dataset. This is when some of the variables are synthesized, and some other variables are retained. This is similar to the approach that is used with traditional de-identification methods. However, with partial synthesis the number of synthesized variables can still be quite large.

When partial synthesis is used, it is recommended that the organization or analyst perform a privacy assurance check on every dataset that is generated. This provides additional assurance that the privacy risks have been managed.

Organizing Data Synthesis

The success of synthetic data generation projects depends on a set of technical and change management factors. Change management is used here to refer to the activities that are needed to support the analyst and analytics leadership in changing their practices to embed the use of synthetic data into their work. The practices we cover in the following sections can have an outsize influence on the outcome of implementing data synthesis.

While the amount of manual effort to synthesize data is relatively small, many data synthesis methods are computationally intensive. Therefore, we first discuss the importance of computing capacity. We next consider the situation in which analysts need to work only with cohorts rather than with full datasets. The section closes with a discussion of the importance of validation studies, initially and continuously, to get and maintain the buy-in of data analysts and data users.

Computing Capacity

Data synthesis and privacy assurance, especially for large and complex datasets, can be computationally intensive. This is especially true for large datasets with many variables and many transactions. One should not underestimate this because the synthesis process can take a long time otherwise. While arguably it is only a matter of time before this problem is solved, there are also some structural issues to consider.

For example, when using decision trees for data synthesis, the number of categories in a data field can be a problem. Decision trees select variables and perform binary splits on them to build the tree. For nominal variables these algorithms evaluate all possible splits. For example, if a variable has three possible values {A, B, C}, then the possible splits are {{A},{B,C}}, {{A,B},{C}}, or {{A,C},{B}}. Each of these is evaluated to find the best split. When there are many categories, the number of possible splits can be very large and computationally infeasible to perform. In such cases, special manipulations of the data during pre-processing are needed to enable the synthesis process to proceed.

These are just some of the practical issues that must be considered during the synthesis process. As you synthesize data, there will be more added to this list depending on the types of data that you are working with.

A Toolbox of Techniques

There are multiple methods that can be used for data synthesis. Some methods are best suited to smaller datasets, whereas others will work well only when the datasets are large and can train a deep learning model. Also, some methods will be better suited to cross-sectional data, and for longitudinal data various approaches can be used, depending on the degree of complexity of the longitudinal sequences.

In practice, unless an organization's datasets are homogeneous, they will need to have a toolbox of synthesizers, with each suited to particular data characteristics. Heuristics can be applied manually or in an automated manner to select the most suitable synthesizer for a particular dataset. Assuming that there is a singular unicorn synthesizer is not going to be the most prudent way to approach the building of data synthesis capacity.

Synthesizing Cohorts Versus Full Datasets

As a practical matter, many data analyses and AIML models are performed or developed, respectively, on specific cohorts or subsets of the full dataset. For example, only a subset of consumers within a specific age range may be of interest or only a subset of the variables. Then that cohort is extracted from the master dataset and sent to the analysts.

For data synthesis, it is much easier to synthesize the full dataset than to synthesize each cohort as it is extracted. The data utility will generally be higher that way, and there is no obvious advantage to the synthesis of individual cohorts.

Given this argument, it is recommended that the data be synthesized as it is coming in rather than as it is going out. For example, if an organization has a data lake and is extracting cohorts from that for specific analyses, then the data synthesis should be performed when the data is going into the data lake such that the data lake consists of only synthetic data.

Continuous Data Feeds

We often see continuous data feeds that need to be synthesized. The common approach is to batch the incoming data, train or update a model with the new data, and then generate a new sequence. Since training does take time, retraining may not have to be performed if there are response-time constraints on the data feeds. In such a case, data can be synthesized using existing models with only periodic updates.

Privacy Assurance as Certification

In the current regulatory environment and with contemporary public discourse that is heavily focused on privacy risks, a prudent organization will err on the conservative side. Regulators' and the public's concerns about privacy risks and the increasingly negative narrative on the secondary uses of data mean that it is important for organizations to perform privacy assurance on their synthetic data. As noted before, it should not be taken for granted that the synthesis models were not overfit—that is an empirical question.

There are a few reasons that regular privacy assurance on synthetic data is important:

- It provides the documentation necessary to demonstrate that the identification risks are very small. Such documentation may become helpful if questions are raised about the uses of secondary data.

- It provides assurance to the data provider that the synthesis process was done well and that the synthesis model did not overfit to the original data.

- It demonstrates to the public a level of due diligence when using data for secondary purposes.

Therefore, as a matter of practice, organizations performing data synthesis should consider incorporating privacy assurance as a standard part of the synthesis workflow.

Performing Validation Studies to Get Buy-In

Perhaps the key factor in the success of data synthesis projects is getting the buy-in of the data users and data analysts. In many instances, the use of synthetic data is new for data analysts, for example. Including validation steps in the process of deploying data synthesis will be important, and we have included that explicitly in the process illustrated in Figure 2-14. Validation means that a number of case studies are performed to demonstrate the utility of the synthetic data for the task at hand. Even if case studies exist in other organizations, demonstrations on an organization's own data can be much more impactful for the data analysts using the synthetic data.

A validation means showing that the results from the synthetic data are similar to the results from the real data. The extent of the similarity will depend on the specific use case. For example, if the use case is to use synthetic data for software testing, then the criteria for similarity would be less stringent than if the data will be used to build an AIML model to identify high-risk insurance claims.

Such validation studies should be chosen to be representative of the datasets and situations that are likely going to be encountered in practice. Choosing the most challenging dataset or context for a validation is not going to be very informative and increases the chances of unsuccessful outcomes. Going in the other direction and choosing the simplest scenarios may not be convincing for the eventual synthetic data users.

Motivated Intruder Tests

Another approach to perform privacy assurance is to organize an attack on the synthetic data to empirically test the extent to which a synthetic record can be mapped to a real person. These are typically called *motivated intruder tests* in the privacy community.

A motivated intruder test mimics the behavior of an adversary who may attempt to identify synthetic data (with some constraints, such as no criminal or unethical behavior). The individual or team performing such a test should be independent of the team that performed the synthesis.

For a motivated intruder test to be effective, there must be a meaningful way to verify a suspected match of a synthetic record with a real person. Since that is not going to be possible with synthetic data, the limitation of this type of test is that it will result only in suspected matches with no ability to verify them.

Who Owns Synthetic Data?

We decided to leave the most controversial question to the end of the last chapter. The question here is who owns synthetic data. Let's say that an insurance company owns a particular claims dataset. If a vendor creates a synthetic variant of that dataset, is the synthetic data still owned by the insurance company?

Part of the answer to this question will depend on the contracts that are in place. Since many existing contracts would not have contemplated data synthesis, it is likely that this issue was not directly addressed.

Because there is no one-to-one mapping between the synthetic records and the real customers of that insurance company, it is not the same data. However, the inferences that can be drawn from the synthetic data would be similar to those from the original data.

We will leave the answering of this question as an exercise for the reader.

Conclusions

In this chapter we touched upon some of the practical challenges and solutions that can occur in a data synthesis project.

After completing this chapter (assuming that you have read all of the previous ones as well) you will have a good understanding of the basic concepts and techniques behind data synthesis, as well as the use cases for synthesis and the types of problems that it can solve. As important, you should now have an appreciation of the balance between privacy protection and data utility in synthetic data.

Index

cumulative density functions (see CDFs)

D

data benchmarks, 17
data cleansing, 41
data complexity, managing, 12, 137-142
data controller–data processor relationship
    under GDPR, 126-128
data flow assessment, 42-46
data frame, defined, 50
data harmonization, 41, 138
data preparation, 41, 42, 138
data quality, assessing prior to synthesis, 41, 141
data shaping versus data preparation, 138
data standardization, 41
data synthesis (see synthetic data generation)
data synthesis pipeline, 42-46
data-access issue (see access to data)
datathons, 16
dates, synthesizing, 140
de-identification of data, 31-32, 34-38, 123, 131
decision criteria for PETs, 28
decision framework for PETs, 33-38
deep learning methods, 107-108
demographic dates, 140
digital health technologies, 13-16
disclosure of data (see identity disclosure)
distinguishability utility metric, 87-92, 103
distribution modeling, 49-67
    classical distributions, 49, 50, 96, 97-98, 101
    fitting process, 50-60, 77
    framing data, 50
    generating synthetic data from distribution,
        62-67
    marginal distributions, 97-99, 103
    multivariate distributions, 61, 96
    to real data, 60-62, 99-103
    univariate distributions, 60-62, 67, 75-77
    unstructured data challenge, 60

E

European Data Protection Board (see Article 29
    Working Party)
event dates, 140
exponential distributions, 97-98, 101

F

factor data, distribution of, 56

factory automation, synthetic data in, 9-11
field types, pre-processing of datasets, 138
financial services case study, 17-19
fitting, defined, 60
    (see also distribution modeling)

G

GAN (generative adversarial network), 107
Gaussian copulas, 98, 102
GBMs (generalized boosted models), 83, 90
GDPR (General Data Protection Regulation), 4,
    31-32, 34-38, 125-129
generalization of locations, 141
generalized boosted models (see GBMs)
generative adversarial network (see GAN)
generic data utility metrics, 70, 74-92
geography, synthesizing, 141
Government Accountability Office, 4

H

harmonization, data, 41, 138
Health Insurance Portability and Accountabil-
    ity Act (see HIPAA)
healthcare case study, 11-16
Hellinger distance, 77
HHP (Heritage Health Prize), 15
HIPAA (Health Insurance Portability and
    Accountability Act), 4, 30-32, 36, 130-133
HIPAA LDS (limited dataset), 30, 31, 36
HIPAA Privacy Rule, 131-132
HIPAA Security Rule, 132
hybrid synthetic data, 103-105

I

identifiability spectrum, 24-25, 27
identity disclosure, 115-136
    attribute, 117-119, 134
    defined, 116
    inferential, 119
    information gain issue, 117, 121
    meaningful, 120
    privacy law impacts on synthetic data,
        123-135
    unique matches, 122
implementation cost criterion for PET deploy-
    ment, 28
implementing data synthesis, 23-48
    data synthesis pipeline, 42

pre- and post-processing steps in data synthesis, 138-142
preparation, data, 41, 42, 138
privacy, 28
    (see also PETs)
    computing capacity to assure, 142
    versus cost and utility, 34-38
    data-access issue, 4, 11-16
    identity disclosure and (see identity disclosure)
    importance of assuring, 144
    legal impacts on synthetic data, 123-135
    motivated intruder tests to assure, 145
    partial synthesis and, 142
    in project process, 40
privacy-enhancing technologies (see PETs)
probability integral transform, 98
probability of identification, factors in, 24, 27
program management, 47-48
propensity score, in distinguishability method, 87-92
protected health information (see PHI)
proxy, synthetic data generation as, 6, 73
pseudonymization, 30, 34-38, 139
public datasets, limitations of, 5

Q

quality of data, assessing prior to synthesis, 41, 141
quasi-identifiers, defined, 122

R

rapid technology evaluation, 14
re-identification risks for data, 12, 18, 115
real data
    CCPA restrictions on, 129-130
    de-identification of data as, 123
    distribution fitting to, 60-62, 101-102
    GDPR restrictions on, 125-129
    HIPAA restrictions and permissions, 131-133
    in hybrid synthetic data generation, 103
    synthesis with and without, 2-3
    versus synthetic, 2, 128
    working with, vii, 39, 41
realistic synthetic data, generating, 99-103
receiver operating characteristics (ROC) curve (see ROC)
relative dates, conversion of event dates to, 140

risk-based de-identification methods, 31, 33-38
robot training, synthetic data in, 9-11
ROC (receiver operating characteristics) curve, 83-85

S

Safe Harbor de-identification PET, 31, 36-38
sales of personal information, CCPA's focus on, 129
scalability of data synthesis, assessment of, 47
secure multiparty computation, 30
sequences, synthesizing, 108-112
sequential machine learning synthesis, 105
shaping of data versus preparation, 138
singling out, Article 29 Working Party definition, 134
software testing, synthetic data use case, 18
spectrum of identifiability, 24-25
STAC-A2 benchmark, 17
standardization of data, 41
structured data, defined, 1
subjective assessments of data utility, 70
synthesis, defined, 1
synthetic data generation
    benefits of, 4-8
    case studies, 8-21
    data complexity, managing, 137-142
    defining, 1-4
    getting started, 49-67
    identity disclosure (see identity disclosure)
    implementing (see implementing data synthesis)
    methods (see methods for generating synthetic data)
    organizing data synthesis, 142-146
    types of, 1-4
    utility evaluation (see utility)

T

temporal data, pre-processing of, 140
text fields, inability to synthesize, 141
theory, generating synthesized data from, 95-99
    copulas with known marginal distributions, 98-99
    in hybrid synthetic data, 103
    inducing correlations with marginal distributions, 97-98
    multivariate normal distribution, 96

third-party service providers, sharing real data
    with, 127, 129, 132
time series data, distribution of, 57-60
timing of implementing data synthesis, 24
transition matrix, synthesizing sequences, 109
transportation case study, 19-21
trust
    consumer trust criterion for PET deploy-
        ment, 28, 37
    versus cost and utility, 33-38
    in synthetic data, 6, 40
trusted third parties, in data synthesis pipeline
    assessment, 42-46

U

unbounded real numbers, data distribution, 50
unique identifiers, processing dataset for syn-
    thesis, 139
unique matches, identity disclosure, 122
univariate distributions, 60-62, 67, 75-77
unstructured data
    defined, 1
    distribution challenge of, 60
US Census Bureau, 7

utility, 69-94
    data synthesis project assessment, 39-41
    defining, 1, 3
    versus privacy and trust, 33-38
    replication of analysis framework, 71-73
    synthetic data as proxy, 6, 73
utility metrics, 74-92
    bivariate statistics comparison, 79-81
    distinguishability, 87-92
    multivariate prediction model comparison,
        83-87
    univariate distribution comparison, 75-77

V

VAE (variational autoencoder), 107
validation studies for buy-in purposes, 144
variable or field in data frame, defined, 50
Vivli-Microsoft Data Challenge, 16

W

workload-aware approach to synthetic data
    evaluation, 70, 71-73

About the Authors

Dr. Khaled El Emam is a senior scientist at the Children's Hospital of Eastern Ontario Research Institute and the director of the multidisciplinary Electronic Health Information Laboratory, conducting applied academic research on synthetic data generation methods and tools, and re-identification risk measurement. He is also a professor in the Faculty of Medicine at the University of Ottawa, Canada.

Khaled is the cofounder of Replica Analytics, a company focused on the development of synthetic data to drive the application of AI and Machine Learning (AIML) in the healthcare industry. He currently invests, advises, and sits on the boards of technology companies developing data protection technologies and building analytics tools to support healthcare delivery and drug discovery.

He has been performing data analysis since the early '90s, building statistical and machine learning models for prediction and evaluation. Since 2004 he has been developing technologies to facilitate the sharing of data for secondary analysis, from basic research on algorithms to applied solutions development that have been deployed globally. These technologies address problems in anonymization and pseudonymization, synthetic data, secure computation, and data watermarking.

He has cowritten and coedited multiple books on privacy and software engineering topics. In 2003 and 2004, he was ranked as the top systems and software engineering scholar in the world by the *Journal of Systems and Software*, based on his research on measurement and quality evaluation and improvement.

Previously, Khaled was a senior research officer at the National Research Council of Canada. He also served as the head of the Quantitative Methods Group at the Fraunhofer Institute in Kaiserslautern, Germany. He held the Canada Research Chair in Electronic Health Information at the University of Ottawa from 2005 to 2015, and has a PhD from the Department of Electrical and Electronics Engineering, King's College, at the University of London, England.

Lucy Mosquera has a background in biology and mathematics, having done her studies at Queen's University in Kingston, Canada and the University of British Columbia. In the past she has provided data management support to clinical trials and observational studies at Kingston General Hospital. She also worked on clinical trial data sharing methods based on homomorphic encryption and secret-sharing protocols with various companies. She is the lead data scientist at Replica Analytics, where she is responsible for integrating her subject area expertise in health data into innovative methods for synthetic data generation and the assessment of that data, as well as overseeing the company's analytics program.

Dr. Richard Hoptroff specializes in technology start-ups based on the artificial intelligence and time series data processing techniques he developed during his PhD. His primary focus is on early-stage development, turning concepts into commercial, buyable products and services while minimizing risk and seed capital. In the last 30 years he has been the founder of start-ups in forecasting software, data mining, Bluetooth radio, ASIC fabrication, high-accuracy smartwatch manufacturing, and Traceable Time as a Service.

Richard studied physics at King's College, at the University of London, England, where he specialized in optical/quantum computing and neural networks, and where he met coauthor Khaled El Emam. He drafted most of his contribution to this book in Bunhill Fields in London, UK, by the resting place of Thomas Bayes.

Colophon

The animal on the cover of *Practical Synthetic Data Generation* is a common potoo (*Nyctibius griseus*), a nocturnal bird native to the tropics of Central and South America. It can be found in forested habitats with scattered trees, such as forest edges along rivers or roadsides.

The common potoo resembles a combination of an owl and a nightjar—it has large, black-striped head and striking yellow eyes. Thanks to its splotchy pattern of gray-brown feathers, the potoo becomes almost completely invisible during the day, perched upright on stumps and dead trees. At night, the potoo uses its small, hooked bill to hunt flying insects, sweeping up moths and beetles with its wide mouth.

The female common potoo does not build a nest but instead lays a single egg, white with purple-brown spots, on top of a stump or in the indent of a broken branch. Typically, the male incubates the egg during the day, while at night those duties are shared between the monogamous parents.

Perhaps best known for its haunting and melancholic song, a *BO-OU, BO-ou, bo-ou, bo-ou, bo-ou, bo-ou, bo-ou, bo-ou* dropping in both pitch and volume, the common potoo is the subject of local folklore. In Peru, for instance, it's said the potoo's call is that of a lost child calling for their mother.

While the common potoo's conservation status is listed as of Least Concern, many of the animals on O'Reilly covers are endangered; all of them are important to the world.

The cover illustration is by Karen Montgomery, based on a black and white engraving from *The English Cyclopedia: Natural History*. The cover fonts are Gilroy Semibold and Guardian Sans. The text font is Adobe Minion Pro; the heading font is Adobe Myriad Condensed; and the code font is Dalton Maag's Ubuntu Mono.

O'REILLY®

There's much more where this came from.

Experience books, videos, live online training courses, and more from O'Reilly and our 200+ partners—all in one place.

Learn more at oreilly.com/online-learning

Milton Keynes UK
Ingram Content Group UK Ltd.
UKHW050345170924
448423UK00007B/88

9 781492 072744